Bloom's Modern Critical Views

Bloom's Modern Critical Views

you or I burn you. Therefore, in the absence of any law, it is preferable to stab a woman suspected of infidelity than to honor the faithful who have passed on. It is a question of having protectors who are likely to forgive homicide, and a thousand cruzados to put on the scales, which explains why justice holds the latter in her hand. Let blacks and hoodlums be punished so that the importance of good example may be upheld. Let people of rank and wealth be honored, without demanding that they pay their debts, that they renounce vengeance or mitigate their hatred. And while the lawsuits are being fought, since certain little irregularities cannot be totally avoided, let there be chicanery, swindling, appeals, formalities, and evasions, so that those likely to gain a just decision will not gain it too readily, and those likely to lose their appeal will not lose it too soon. In the meantime teats are milked for that delicious milk, money, those rich curds, prime cheese, and a tasty morsel for the bailiff and the solicitor, for the witness and the judge;

Saramago's Swiftian irony will become subtler in later books, but one is dazzled by its pungency here, with that marvelous, pragmatic motto for the Inquisition: "Either I stab you or I burn you." We are not quite in the United States of the second George Bush or in contemporary Portugal, but the implications are there. A great moment comes when the lovers and Padre Lourenço take off together in the Passarolo. As they descend, Saramago invokes the image of Camões, the heroic one-eyed national warrior-epic poet:

Who knows what dangers await them, what Adamastor they will encounter, what Saint Elmo's fires they will see rise from the sea, what columns of water will suck in the air only to expel it once it has been settled? Then Blimunda asks where are we going. And the priest replies: where the arm of the Inquisition cannot reach us if such a place exists.

They come down in the mountains, and Lourenço disappears. Baltasar and Blimunda make their way to his parents' home, where eventually Scarlatti will come to tell them that Padre Bartholomew, pursued by the Inquisition, escaped to Spain and then died in Toledo. Poor Baltasar is impressed into a work crew to build a great Franciscan convent. When he gets free again, he finds and flies in the Passarolo. Meanwhile, poor

Blimunda, who is being raped by a properly pious friar, kills him with the detachable spike that Baltasar usually wears. For nine long years, Blimunda searches for her Baltasar, and finds him already burning in a glorious act-of-faith involving the usual collection of Jews, playwrights, and similar riff-raff.

Then Blimunda said: Come. The will of Baltasar Sete-Sóis broke free from his body, but did not ascend to the stars, for it belonged to the earth and to Blimunda. Though this is a marvelous aesthetic conclusion, it leaves us a little sad. What can happen next? Perhaps Blimunda will find the Passarola and use Baltasar's will for a final flight, but she will be alone in a melancholy freedom, wherever she lands, if ever she lands. Portugal in the early 18th century has yielded us the following. The country is Hell, governed by a viciously stupid royal family, and tortured incessantly by a Church indistinguishable from the Inquisition. What saves it from hellishness? Only four beings: the partly Jewish witch Blimunda; the heroic, Cervantes-like one-armed soldier, Baltasar; the inventor of the Passarolo, Padre Lourenço, who converts to the unitive God of Judaism, and then goes off to die in Spain; and the survivor, Domenico Scarlatti, who will go on playing his ethereal melodies that alone redeem such a world. Saramago prophetically consigns Portugal, the Catholic Church and the monarchy to the hell of history. The Passarola, image of illusory freedom, saves no one, and its great inventor exiles himself to die in Toledo. Our lovers never totally lose one another and what redeems the book is Saramago's real love for them, which transcends all his ironies. I pass to the wonderful irreality of *The Year of the Death of Ricardo Reis* (1984). We are in Hell again, that is to say historical Portugal in December 1935, with Salazar come to power, and Spain about to endure the Fascist usurpation. Acts of faith will be performed by machine guns and rifles, less pleasant to God than the aroma of burning flesh. Our hero is the amiable poet, Dr. Ricardo Reis, one of Pessoa's heteronyms: a mild, Horatian Epicurean, who has returned from Brazil to Lisbon. He checks into his hotel, and then goes out to read a newspaper that reports the death of Fernando Pessoa, and naturally pays a visit of respect to his creator's tomb. Already we have had allusions to Eça and to Borges: we are in the reality of the fabulists and poets.

Ricardo Reis pursues two erotic quests, an idealized one for Marcenda, paralyzed in her left hand, and a fleshly one with Lydia, the hotel chambermaid. But first he returns from dinner, to find the ghostly Pessoa waiting for him in his hotel room, and they converse like the old friends they are. They will go on meeting, since ghosts have eight months of freedom, and in the meantime Lydia enters the bed of Ricardo Reis.

Though Salazar's Portugal is always in the background, we essentially are in a pleasant realm: literary, erotic, nostalgic. I pause to note that I know no other novelistic atmosphere at all like the ambiance of *The Year of the Death of Ricardo Reis*. It is an utterly new mode of aestheticism: both visionary and realistic, the cosmos of the great poet Pessoa and of the Fascist dictator Salazar and yet it presents us also with an original literary enigma: how long can Ricardo Reis survive the death of Fernando Pessoa? For three hundred and fifty pages we have experienced the life and loves of a heteronym. What a triumph for Pessoa, and for Saramago. The novel's beautifully modulated closing passage has an utterly unprecedented tonality:

> As they left the apartment, Fernando Pessoa told him, you forgot your hat. You know better than I do that hats aren't worn where we're going. On the sidewalk opposite the park, they watched the pale lights flicker on the river, the ominous shadows of the mountains. Let's go then, said Fernando Pessoa. Let's go, agreed Ricardo Reis. Adamastor did not turn around to look, perhaps afraid that if he did, he might let out finally his mighty howl. Here, where the sea ends and the earth awaits.

The will of Baltasar belonged to Blimunda and the earth, and the earth awaits both poets, Pessoa and Reis. The earth is always waiting for us in Saramago; at the close of his magnificent fantasy, *The Stone Raft* (1986), we are gently assured: "The elm branch is green. Perhaps it will flower again next year." The book's epigraph quotes the great Cuban fabulist, Alejo Carpentier, who is of Saramago's school: "Every future is fabulous." In Carpentier, yes, but in Saramago, these things are ordered differently. That elm branch starts all the trouble anyway, and converts Iberia into a stone raft, after Joana Carda scratches the ground with it, having no idea it was a magic wand. The genius of Saramago is off and running, fulfilling its destiny of disturbing us into a fuller realization of what it means to read and to write.

It would madden me, and all of us, if I attempted to summarize this sublimely zany narrative. Its given is summary enough; the entire slab of Spain and Portugal has spun loose from Europe, and heads out into the Atlantic. Saramago's aesthetic burden therefore is immense; if you start your story with *that*, how are you to catch up to yourself? I retract; there is no aesthetic burden for the cunning Saramago. We never get at all far from that original outrage. It is almost halfway through the novel, on page 127, that Joanna Carda explains why and how the catastrophe happened? She required a symbolic act to indicate that she was separating from her husband: They are standing on the edge of the clearing, Joana Carda detains the men a bit longer, these are her final words, I picked up the stick from the ground, the wood seemed to be living as if it were the whole tree from which it had been cut, or rather this is what I now feel as it comes back to me, and at that moment, with a gesture more like a child's than an adult's, I drew a line that separated me forever from Coimbra and the man with whom I lived, a line that divided the world into two halves, as you can see from here.

They advanced to the middle of the clearing, drew close, there was the line, as clear as if it had just been drawn, the earth piled up on either side, the bottom layer still damp despite the warmth of the sun. They remain silent, the men are at a loss for words, Joana Carda has nothing more to say, this is the moment for a daring gesture that could make a mockery of her wonderful tale. She drags one foot over the ground, smooths the soil as if she were using a level, stamps on it and presses down, as if committing an act of sacrilege. The next moment, before the astonished gaze of all the onlookers, the line reappears, it looks exactly as it was before, the tiny particles of soil, the grains of sand resume their previous shape and form, return to where they were before, and the line is back. Between the part that was obliterated and the rest, between one side and the other, there is no visible difference. Her nerves on edge, Joana Carda says in a shrill voice, I've already swept away the entire line, I've covered it with water, yet it keeps reappearing, try for yourselves if you wish, I even put stones on top, and when I removed them the line was still there, why don't you try if you still need convincing.

Nothing works; she is accurate. When then is to be done? Saramago, who is the Devil, is not so much making fun of Europe, or even of Nato or the European Community, but of the ultimate ideas of the geopolitical, the geological, and of all related fantasies that pass as realities. By page 139. he is in a hilarious ecstasy:

> Let us wage that we will ultimately be reduced to a single nation, the quintessence of the European spirit, a single and perfect sublimation, Europe, namely, Switzerland.

The joke, once started cannot be stopped. The late J.F.K. is permanently repaid for his "Ich bin ein Berliner" when all Europe is swept by the slogan: *We also are Iberians*. Anarchist outrages follow, as millions of youths repeat the Great Awakening of the late 1960's, smashing TV stations and shop-fronts, turning Europe into Seattle: For the catalogs of memoirs and reminiscences there remained those dying words of the handsome young Dutchman hit by a rubber bullet ... At last, I'm Iberian, and with these words he expired ...

Except for Joana Carda, I have not mentioned the three other early protagonists, and don't really want to, because they are mere males and they do not seem as important as the curious dog who tags along throughout. Or rather, they tag along, as only the dog seems to know where they are going. One of them, José Anaiço, is taken, by Joana Carda. Another, Joaquim Sassa, will be selected by Maire Guavaira, to whose house the dog leads them. That leaves Pedro Orce, who is closest to the wise dog, whose name sometimes in Pilot. Now that everyone has a home, the peninsula's dilemma remains: Portugal is rushing towards the Azores. In a general time of anxiety and exodus, we now see that Saramago has constructed an oasis, where two women, three men, a dog, and now also a horse, live in perfect harmony. Fortunately, Iberia alters course, and there is no disaster, and the little group (the dog now named Constant) waits to see whether they will surge on to join Canada or the United States.

Sadly, our little community falls out, for a time, even as Portugal and Spain drift towards North America. But the peninsula begins to move away, and rotate, and Pedro Orce dies, and everyone weeps, the dog included. He is buried, the dog Ardent departs, the peninsula has stopped, and the two couples will continue on their wanderings, carrying the elm branch with them.

This rugged narrative does not want to be interpreted, nor should we be tactless, but I will hover round it, as Werner Herzog keeps our eyes circling his raft in *Aguirre the Wrath of God* (my favorite movie, with Klaus Kinski as Aguirre as Kinski). We don't ever see why Joana should want José Anaiço, whose only salient quality is that he activates starlings, or again why Maria takes Sassa, whose role as stone-thrower into oceans hardly seems enough to individuate him. Pedro Orce has the Hemingwayesque ability to kick up earth-tremblings, but all it gets him is the dog. The book-long hegira of the group cannot sustain interpretation or rather interprets itself as a sustained irony. At least these men and women are not going to become the unctuous Portuguese prime-minister, who drones on exhorting the noble Portuguese to be steadfast while he secretly entreats Galicia to come over to Portugal. The Church, after being obliterated in *Baltasar and Blimunda* and *The Year of the Death of Ricardo Reis*, is largely ignored in *The Stone Raft*, presumably because Saramago was preserving his firepower for the Christian God in *The Gospel According to Jesus Christ* (1991).

The Gospel, as I've said already, seems to me Saramago upon his heights, but as I've written about it elsewhere at some length I want here only to admire its sexual love affair between Jesus Christ and Mary Magdalene, which is the most poignant and persuasive of all Saramago's High Romantic couplings. It breathes authentic ardour; read it side-by-side with the roughly similar matter in D.H. Lawrence's *The Man Who Died*, and Saramago will win the palm.

I have passed over my personal favorite in Saramago, *The History of the Siege of Lisbon* (1989), because I want to dwell awhile in this magnificent demonstration that there is no history, only biography, as Emerson polemically assured us. Saramago, more pugnaciously, tells us that there is no history, only fiction, but Emerson hardly would have been bothered, since for him fiction was only another mask for biography. I add the assertion of the divine Oscar Wilde, which is that the highest criticism is the only form of autobiography that avoids vulgarity. Fusing Emerson, Saramago, and Wilde I joyously join in *The History of the Siege of Lisbon*.

In 1147 the King of Portugal took Lisbon back from the Moors with significant aid from Crusaders, European knights battling at the Church's summons. Raimundo Silva, a proofreader, audaciously revises this history, so that only the Portuguese King retakes his own capital. Though I regard *The Gospel According to Jesus Christ* as Saramago's masterwork to date, I love *The History of the Siege of Lisbon* best among his books because it is the most light-hearted. *The Stone Raft* is crossed by the irony of Europe's hypocrisies, and *The Year of the Death of Ricardo Reis* is a parable of the triumph of Iberian Fascism. *Baltasar and Blimunda* is properly full of scorn of Church and Kingdom, but that also curbs exuberance. The later books—*Blindness* and *All the Names*—are dark works, though to very different degrees. For me the heart of Saramago is *The History of the Siege of Lisbon*, possibly because it communicates so freely Saramago's own pleasure in his work. But, going on seventy-one, I am willing to be sentimental. The love-story of Raimundo Silva and Maria Sara is sweet, not bittersweet. It breathes wholeheartedness, and is gentler, easier to linger with than the sublime embrace of Mary Magdalene and God's victimized son, Jesus Christ. Both Raimundo and Maria Sara are weather-beaten, and the mutual love that comes to them is an enchantment for the reader, whoever she or he is.

But I digress to Saramago's *Journey to Portugal* (1990), which arrived in the midst of this meditation, and gives me a more personal insight into someone whom I regard as our planet's strongest living novelist, beyond any contemporary European or any of the Americans, whether they write in English, Spanish, or Portuguese. *Journey to Portugal* pursues the nation's culture and history, but as only the living eminence of that culture could seek it. The traveller is like William Blake's Mental Traveller, who makes the observations of a visionary. An American reviewer, long resident in Portugal, deprecated Saramago's *Journey*, saying it was not useful, but it does not take a great imaginer to compose a guide-book. Like Blake, Saramago sees *through* the eye, not with it. The traveler gives us the spiritual form of Portugal: a compound of culture and history with what only the inner eye can behold. Sometimes, in reading *Journey to Portugal*, I am haunted by subtly complex intimations of the dark novel of 1995, the disturbing fantasy called *Blindness*. Only so comprehensive and searching a seer would turn, years later, to such a fantasy. To see so much, and so well, is to anticipate the terrors and yet also the dignity of loss.

The concept of dignity returns me to the love of Maria Sara and Raimundo, and to the humane comedy of *The History of the Siege of Lisbon*. This is the most charming of Saramago's books; the novelist himself is so moved by the love of Raimundo and Maria Sara that he all but abdicates social satire, though his genius for irony manifests itself incessantly. Whenever I seek to introduce friends or students to Saramago, I suggest they begin with *The Siege of Lisbon*, surely a fiction that every sensitive reader of good will would embrace.

The Gospel According to Jesus Christ (1991) changed these notes to that of cosmological tragedy. Saramago's Jesus, his God, his devil: all are open to interpretation, including Saramago's own, with which I do not always agree. Myself a Jewish Gnostic by persuasion, I am delighted by the hangman God of Saramago's *Gospel*, but I suspect that Saramago may agree with his own Christ's benign farewell to the heavenly father: "Men, forgive Him, for He knows not what He has done." If that is not irony, what is it?

The *Gospel*, in my reading, stands apart among Saramago's fictions, partly because of its aesthetic eminence, yet also because I cannot locate Saramago in it. He has always, as narrator, been his own best character: both in and out of his work, and watching and wondering at it. But where he stands in his *Gospel* seems disputable. "He stands with his Jesus Christ" might be the answer, but only extends the question. The *Gospel's* God is certainly worthy of denial: he is the unpleasantest person in all of Saramago. But here I am perhaps at odds with Saramago and would prefer that anyone interested consult my extended essay on the *Gospel*.

Blindness (1995) reminds us again of Saramago's uncanny power as a fabulist, but also as an imaginative moralist. Nothing in contemporary fiction reveals so clearly the contingent nature of our social realities. Saramago's deepest insight is that our mundane existence is profoundly fragile, dependent upon givens that may be withdrawn any instant. If I compare *Blindness* with *The Plague* by Camus, I find I favor Saramago. Whether or not intentional, the open nature of the allegory in *Blindness* allows the reader to wonder if this is not another parable of the perpetual possibility of the return of Fascism, or of its first advent. As with the *Gospel*, this austere masterpiece is too complex for simple summary, and I hope to write of it elsewhere.

Saramago's Portuguese is still too difficult for me, and so I eagerly await the English translation of his *Caverno*. I close here with a brief coda on *All the Names* (1997), his closest approach to Kafka, though light years from Kafka's "Plenty of hope, for God, but not for us." Senhor José, clerkiest of clerks, quests for an unknown woman, who alas is dead. And that is all. And that is far from all, for since you only can love what you cannot ever know, completely, Senhor José cannot abandon the quest. Perhaps not Kafka, but a curious blend of Robert Louis Stevenson and Melville, might be the paradigm, but the vision of Saramago has Borgesian elements in it, and these precursors are folded in a single flame.

The Registrar, for whom Senhor José works, seems to me less God than he is Saramago himself, teaching men and women of letters that: "we who write and manipulate the papers of life and death should reunite the dead and living in one single archive." As a literary critic, I take heart from the wisdom of Saramago. For what am I but one of the last Defenders of the Old Aesthetic Faith, the trust in the Covenant between the writers of genius and the discerning reader?

RICHARD A. PRETO-RODAS

A View of Eighteenth-Century Portugal: José Saramago's Memorial do convento (Baltsar and Blimunda)

In a recent interview José Saramago stressed that his novel *Memorial do convento* (1983) represents an attempt to examine certain persistent traits in Portuguese culture.[1] According to the author, the plot's eighteenth-century setting has had far greater impact on his nation's current status than has the more-studied sixteenth century. The results of his portrayal of the roots of contemporary Portugal are hardly flattering, but his attempt certainly has produced an extraordinary work. *Memorial do convento* won the first prize of the PEN Club of Portugal in 1983, it has already been issued in a Brazilian edition, and it further consolidates Saramago's place in Portuguese letters. The following commentary is intended to suggest why Saramago's most recent contribution to the Portuguese literary scene is a major one.

The central event in *Memorial do convento* is the construction of an enormous monument to religious and royal pride, the Convent of Mafra, comprising several wings housing a basilica, a palace, an abbey, and other *dependências*. For Saramago, as for other like-minded predecessors who have commented on Dom João V's grandiose project, the convent represents the triumph of obscurantism and its attendant forces of waste, ignorance, corruption, and religious fanaticism. No less persistent in Portuguese history, however, has been the kind of critical outlook and independence of spirit which account for a lesser-known event of the period: the experiments

From *World Literature Today*, vol. 61, no. 1 (Winter 1987). © 1986 by the University of Oklahoma Press.

1

of the Brazilian-born priest Bartolomeu Lourenço de Gusmão with the idea of an airborne vehicle. Saramago contrasts these two enterprises throughout his novel, so that the convent becomes the expression of the dead weight of reactionary absolutism while the flying machine embodies the aspirations of a few to soar above the limitations of their time.

The author has not written a traditional historical novel with the genre's pretensions to creating the illusion of a self-contained era. Rather, his intention is to underscore the oppressive limitations of eighteenth-century Portuguese society by assuming the voice of the self-conscious narrator who tells his story with an eye cocked on the twentieth century. Throughout *Memorial do convento* the author strikes a mocking tone as he subjects the foibles and vanities of Dom João V's court to the caustic vision and ironic wit of a modern-day rationalist. The mockery is not one-sided, however, for we are frequently reminded that recent history in Portugal betrays uncomfortable similarities to the time that Saramago has re-created. It is the society described by Voltaire as one where "festivities were religious processions, palaces were monasteries, and the king's mistress was a nun."[2] For all their patronage of operas and harpsichord recitals, the absolute monarchy and the Church had created a world which another French contemporary describes as "tout à fait triste."[3] Saramago's success in providing a fascinating literary experience despite his subject's unrelieved grim sadness is a tribute to his skill.

The author gains our acceptance of his ironic point of view by assuming the voice of a genial and cordial raconteur who tells his tale with frequent asides, digressions, and comments, all of which blend with the narrative proper and the characters' dialogues. Saramago attributes his technique to a brainstorm which revealed that *oralidade* or the stance of a storyteller would best allow the narrator to be everywhere heard, now in his own words and now in the dialogues, which are not set off or distinguished by punctuation.[4] The reader is thus obliged to read "aloud," thereby re-creating the oral character of *Memorial do convento*. Considerable effort is required to "listen" to an account which shifts without signals from one focal point to another while one character's speech merges with another's and with the narrator's own voice.

The opening chapter provides the inciting moment, sets the scene, and sounds the tone which accompanies the reader to the very end. The august personages that are Dom João V and his Austrian queen Dona Maria Ana are introduced in all their splendor. In emulation of his model, France's "Sun King" Louis XIV, Dom João lives a life of high theatre, where even his regular conjugal visits to the chamber of his childless consort take on the solemn character of a sacramental ritual. Reality of a lesser order is suggested by references to the bedbugs which infest the imposing four-poster, whose regal occupants sweat and reek in royal rutting.

The king's desire for an heir is perhaps second to his wish for a Portuguese equivalent to the basilica of St. Peter in the Vatican, a model of which he frequently assembles and dismantles before the reverential admiration of his court. A vow to construct an even greater monument in Mafra should an heir be conceived is followed one night by an especially promising coupling. The king then drifts off to dreams which meld his sexual prowess with visions of soaring ecclesiastical towers—all, of course, to the greater glory of God. The narrator concedes that an association of sex and piety is unusual ("Such a personality is not common among kings"), but he reminds us that "Portugal has always been well served with the like" (18).

The startling juxtaposition of religious fervor and royal pomp with crude sensuality and squalor is central to the late-baroque atmosphere of Portugal as shown in *Memorial do convento*. Lisbon, the seat of the empire, is a pigsty whose inhabitants suffer from bad water and wretched social conditions. We are reminded of the technique of a Quevedo as Saramago describes a capital of shocking disparities.

> This city, more than any other, is a mouth that chews too much on one side and too little on the other, there being as a consequence no happy mean between an abundance of double chins on the one hand and scrawny necks on the other, between rosy noses and consumptive nostrils, between the ballerina's buttock and the droopy behind, between the full paunch and the stomach which sticks to one's back. (27)

The constant religious processions afford ladies on balconies with strange thrills ("which only much later will we learn to regard as sadistic," 29) as they watch their lovers below flagellate themselves in bloody penance. The ubiquity of religious observance is matched only by the total absence of any kindness, sympathy, or charity. Commenting on an instance of a father's savage revenge to defend his honor, a veteran of military combat observes that "there is more charity in war" (47).

The veteran is Baltasar Mateus, a penniless twenty-six-year-old from Mafra who has returned from the Spanish frontier, where he lost a hand in defense of his country's impossible causes. His arrival in Lisbon coincides with an auto-da-fé, a lavish spectacle which vies, we are told, with bullfighting in popularity. The narrator releases a torrent of description to convey the excitement and anticipation as throngs flock to the Rossio to witness the Inquisition's grandest show of might in the name of religious right. Alongside Baltasar stand Bartolomeu Lourenço de Gusmão and a comely young woman, Blimunda, who mournfully watches as her mother passes with other penitents about to be exiled to Angola. Mother and daughter are endowed with powers that expose them to the suspicion of orthodoxy's guardians. As the older woman draws abreast of the three young people, who fail to share the mob's excitement, she entrusts her daughter to the maimed veteran with a mere glance and passes on. The young couple recognize in each other kindred souls. Like the priest Gusmão, they are also freethinking skeptics, in but not of their time. Their mutual dedication is immediate and complete, and the three depart the frenzied scene as friends and confidants.

Bartolomeu de Gusmão enlists his fellow dissidents in his experiments to construct a flying machine, a daring venture that would bring him before the Inquisition, were it not for royal support. Even so, he is the target of jibes and satire,[5] and even the king's interest is tenuous, since it rests less on scientific curiosity than on a childish infatuation with the possibility of a new toy. The three, then, decide to conduct their work in a secret workshop on an abandoned estate. Their decision is made as the queen gives birth and the king prepares to fulfill his vow. The antithesis is thus established: on one side we find a daring new invention built by a trio of independent spirits; on the other there is the projected convent-palace which will further consolidate state and Church, thereby driving an already impoverished society even deeper into debt.

Saramago departs from the historical record, which tells of Bartolomeu de Gusmão's experiments with hot-air balloons. Instead, the narrator speaks of a far more marvelous gondola in the shape of a bird, a *passarola*, which will be lifted by two thousand human wills and all their desires and aspirations. As the faculty whereby man hopes to transcend limitations, the will allows one to aspire to soar into space. Thus, by ringing the passarola with tiny amber spheres containing such hopes and aspirations, the contraption will be lifted by the sun's rays. The task of harnessing such an elusive power falls to Blimunda, the seer who, when fasting, can see in others the small dark cloud which is the will. She is to capture in small amber phials the principle of flight at the moment when an individual expires, a common occurrence in a city as plagued by epidemic as is eighteenth-century Lisbon.

The narrator occasionally refers to flight heavenward as the only relief from the wretched realities of the time. One such instance concerns a bloody bullfight attended by an audience of court drones. Part of the festivities includes releasing doves banded with poetic conceits. Although most of the birds fall into the clutches of shrieking ladies-in-waiting, a few "escape ... and climb, climb ... until they reflect on high the sun's light, and when they disappear above the rooftops, they are birds of gold" (99–100). Not every instance of flight from grim reality, however, involves birds or supernatural powers. The narrator tells of several brief interludes of happiness when the intrepid inventor and his friends are joined by a fourth dissenter, the musician Domenico Scarlatti. The Italian is grateful for some enlightened company and brings his harpsichord to the workshop, where he plays while his friends prepare the sails, bellows, and rudder for the *passarola*. His musical skill enchants and uplifts their spirits, and Blimunda observes that if the contraption flies, then "all heaven will be music" (178).

The project is finally completed after a hiatus during which the priest studies physics in Holland and the lovers reside with Baltasar's parents in Mafra, where everyone works on the convent. One afternoon, however, the Inquisition is alerted to the priest's heretical inclinations, and the trio flee in the *passarola*, soaring toward the sun. On the ground is their only witness, Scarlatti. The narrator captures the exhilaration of the experience, which includes flying over the construction site at Mafra before landing at sunset in a mountain thicket a day's walk from the convent. Deranged with fear of the Inquisition, Bartolomeu flees the scene, leaving Blimunda and Baltasar to conceal their invention and return to the poverty and drudgery of living and working on the convent at Mafra. Two visionaries in a land of mean-spirited religiosity, they lead a secretive life. Their coconspirator has fled to Spain, and a dejected Scarlatti returns to his more-tolerant homeland. Better times are a long way off, the narrator reminds us: "Before movie films become a reality, two hundred years must yet pass, to a time when there will be motorized *passarolas*; time weighs heavy while one waits for happiness" (219).

The years pass, the convent nears completion, and the couple guard their secret, occasionally returning to the *passarola* to keep it in repair and under cover lest the sun attract the amber spheres into new flight. On the day in 1727 that the king's monument is to be dedicated, Baltasar returns to the hidden site alone and, while mending the sails, stumbles, tearing away the cover. The sun's rays flood the spheres, and he is lifted to the skies. A desperate Blimunda later comes in search of her lover and immediately surmises what has occurred. The last chapter relates her travels across Portugal in vain search of her Baltasar. Blimunda's quest ends one afternoon in Lisbon when she arrives as an auto-da-fé is in progress. There in the Rossio among eleven victims at the stake including the playwright Antonio José da Silva, "O Judeu"—she spies the blackened shape of Baltasar. With his

expiring breath his will takes flight and finds refuge in the bosom of his
beloved Blimunda.

In a brief summary of *Memorial do convento*, little can be said of such
pertinent aspects as characterization and style. Thus, much could be written
about the inventor-priest's progression from cautious skeptic to freethinker
in constant dread of the Inquisition, and the portrayal of Blimunda and
Baltasar is remarkably free of any sexism. Also, the author's extraordinary
lexical nuance deserves future analysis. No account of the novel, however,
can omit the constant presence of the great construction at Mafra. The
passarola and its hapless builders acquire their full significance thanks to the
opposing forces which are synthesized in the fulfillment of Dom João's vow.
The author succeeds admirably in suggesting the staggering sacrifices so
blithely ignored by the typical guidebook. For Saramago, Mafra symbolizes
a crucial moment in his country's history and presages its subsequent
unhappy development to our own time. His perspective, then, rests firmly on
the tradition of the Cavaleiro de Oliveira, Oliveira Martins, and others who
lament the monkish character of traditional Portuguese officialdom and its
indifference to reality and the crying needs of Portuguese society as it
pursues extravagant follies in defense of outmoded ideologies.[6]

Even in the court of Dom João some voices questioned official values
and indifference to sound national policy. Thus, the British ambassador Lord
Tyrawley observed that, because of Mafra, national life was paralyzed for a
generation as half the country's revenues were expended on the construction
(*P*, 184). Tens of thousands of men from all areas of Portugal were pressed
into service to work night and day so that a king's vow might be fulfilled and
a queen might present her confessor with a new abbey. Others noted that the
riches of an empire, primarily the gold of Brazil, were transformed into the
stone and mortar of Mafra (*P*, 185). What little remained went to developed
European countries, primarily England, which, as Oliveira Martins noted,
fed and clothed a Portuguese society unable to see to its own needs. The
Portuguese historian quotes the royal secretary as complaining, "Monkery
absorbs us, monkery drains everything, monkery is our ruination."[7] With a
few exceptions, life outside the court and ecclesiastical circles was a daily
struggle "in depopulated provinces which are brutalized and wretched" (*H*,
437).

The narrator of *Memorial do convento* often employs the technique of
enumeration to express just how the construction absorbs the wealth of an
empire, from Macao and Goa ("silks ... tea ... rubies ... cinnamon") to
Mozambique and Angola ("blacks ... ivory ... hides") and Brazil ("sugar ...
emeralds ... gold," 227–28). Since Portugal itself lay in abject backwardness

("this poor land of illiterates, rustics, and crude craftsmen"), Dom João's project is entrusted to the rest of Europe, which commands a handsome price.

> The architect is a German ... Italians are the foremen for the carpenters ... businessmen from England, France, Holland ... sell us on a daily basis ... imported from Rome, Venice, Milan, and Genoa, and from Liège and France and Holland, the bells and the carillons, and the lamps, the chandeliers, the candlesticks, the bronze candleholders, and the chalices ... and the statues of saints. (228–29)

The enumeration becomes a torrent and a veritable inventory of Mafra's monument. Every entry becomes an accusation, and wit and caustic irony do not always transform the narrator's anger.

From poor Portugal "let the only requests be for stone, bricks, and wood to burn, and men for the heavy work, not much science" (228). Lord Tyrawley's reference to thousands of toilers often forceably separated from their families suggests none of the courage and simple heroism that Saramago attributes to the real builders of the convent. Indeed, the British observer dismisses the populace's docility with references to a general indifference to reality, as half the country awaits the return of Dom Sebastião and the other half, descendants of Jewish forebears, bides its time until the coming of the Messiah (*H*, 444).

Saramago's sympathies are clearly with the ignored *povo* in his portrayal of the period. Throughout *Memorial do convento* there are names and capsule biographies for the otherwise anonymous thousands who fought in the wars and labored on the royal project. To be sure, their stories vary little, since for the most part they are unschooled peasants, from Minho to the Algarve, already accustomed to physical labor in primitive conditions. Their meager salary and poor diet are small compensation for leaving home and crops in service to Church and Crown. They are shrewd critics of their time and cut through official clichés with a lucidity that provokes admiration in the narrator, who comments, "How such thoughts occur to these rustics, illiterates all, ... that is something we don't understand" (238). Their female counterparts are similarly inclined toward a spirit of quiet rebellion. Whereas others may flock to the convent's dedication, at least one worker's wife, mindful of her husband's suffering, curses the monks en route to their new home with "Damn the monks!" (325). Blimunda's own independence of spirit is dramatically revealed when she kills a friar who attempts to rape her after Baltasar's disappearance.

The heroic character of the *povo* is underscored by Saramago's occasional use of epic style. Indeed, the construction itself provides grist for epic parody, and Camões is paraphrased when courtiers congratulate Dom João on the occasion of the convent's inauguration: "You will tell me which is the greater glory, to be the king of the earth, or the king of these people" (289). There is little ironic humor, however, in another borrowing from *Os Lusíadas*, where we hear the women lament as they watch their men marched off to forced labor: "One of them, her head uncovered [cries], 'Oh sweet, beloved husband,' while another protests, 'Oh my son, my only refuge and sweet succor for my weary old age,'" and an old peasant becomes a second Velho do Restelo, who cries, "Oh, glory of power, oh empty greed, oh infamous king, oh unjust fatherland," until a guard lays him low with a blow to the head (293).

Epic themes and technique especially abound in the seventeenth chapter, which recounts how four hundred oxen and six hundred men transport a gigantic piece of granite to serve as the abbey's veranda. For several miles along twisting mountain trails the workers push, pull, sweat, and curse as they guide the thirty-one-ton slab. One loses a foot, another his life. Today the stone simply serves as a source of statistical pride for guides to impress tourists before passing on to the next attraction: "Ladies and gentlemen, let us now proceed to the next room, for we still have lots to cover" (245). Not a word is said of the Herculean efforts expended so that a king could fulfill his vow: "Here go six hundred men who impregnated no queen with a son, and yet they're the ones who fulfill the vow; they get screwed, if you'll pardon the anachronistic expression" (257).

The narrator acknowledges that the ragged, sweaty crowd—many, like Baltasar, with one handicap or another—hardly measure up to typical heroes, who are "comely and handsome ... trim and straight ... whole and sound" (242). He is no less moved, however, to sing the glory of these valiant wretches: "For this do we write ... to render them immortal." He proceeds, therefore, to compose an ABC of heroic-sounding names like Alcino and Juvino and Marcolino in order to immortalize all the Antónios, Josés, and Manuéis. As always, Saramago avoids falling into facile sentimentality or rhetorical bombast by maintaining a perspective filtered through wry humor and irony. The reader-listener is hardly surprised to encounter an occasional echo of reference to Fernando Pessoa, the Portuguese era's master of literary irony in the modern era.[8]

Saramago's experiment with *oralidade* as found in *Memorial do convento* is eminently successful in conferring unity upon an extraordinarily dense work. The narrator's presence never falters, and the bite and insight of his wit, coupled with a lively style and understanding of a period and its consequences, provide an experience which enriches in every way. The author blends the realism of historical re-creation and the rationalism of a critical perspective with a wealth of cultural references and a fertile imagination open to magic and marvel as antidotes to misery and folly. For the reader-listener the result is a literary tour de force and wonderfully exemplifies the Horatian ideal of profitable pleasure through artistic creation.

NOTES

1. "Nosso hoje se radica muito mais no século XVIII do que no século XVI," as quoted in *Viagem à literatura portuguesa contemporânea* by Cremilda de Araújo Medina, Rio de Janeiro, Nórdica, 1983, p. 264. For a review of *Memorial do convento*, see *WLT* 58:1 (Winter 1984), p. 78.

2. See Hellmut and Alice Wohl, *Portugal*, New York, Scala, 1983, p. 183. All subsequent references use the abbreviation *P*.

3 As quoted in Oliveira Martins, *História de Portugal*, 14th ed., Lisbon, Guimarães, 1964, p. 444. All subsequent references use the abbreviation *H*.

4. "Precisava escrever como se tivesse de contar a história. Percebeu em um instante de lucidez plena, que aquele era um projecto de oralidade." See Araújo Medina, p. 265.

5. Bartolomeu Lourenço de Gusmão's most vociferous detractors were the poets Tomás Pinto Brandão and Pedro de Azevedo Tojal. The latter especially satirizes "O Voador," as the would-be flier was called, in the mock epic *O foguetário*. See Hernâni Cidade, *Lições de cultura e literatura portuguesa*, Coimbra, Coimbra Editora, 1959, vol. 2, p. 298.

6. See Aquilino Ribeiro, *O Cavaleiro de Oliveira*, Porto, Lelo, 1935, and Oliveira Martins, pp. 436–57 ("As Minas do Brasil"), where one finds many references to incidents and data which are incorporated into *Memorial do convento*.

7. Alexandre de Gusmão (no relation to Bartolomeu Lourenço), as quoted in Oliveira Martins, p. 440.

8. On p. 184 Saramago evokes a night scene by quoting from Pessoa's "Vem, noite antiquíssima," and on p. 227 the author refers to the poet's portrayal of Prince Henry the Navigator as seen in *Mensagem*.

MARY L. DANIEL

Symbolism and Synchronicity:
José Saramago's Jangada de Pedra
(The Stone Raft)

Since time immemorial, the Portuguese have traveled, as if by inherent compulsion. They have opened new intercontinental routes "por mares nunca dantes navegados" and been the agents of international commerce and cultural interchange during their Golden Age of navigation. Their fascination with the world "out there" has been balanced by their delight in rediscovering "the world at home," as Almeida Garrett's *Viagens na minha terra* (1843) so gently reminds us. But what of the Portugal of the twentieth century? Are there any new worlds to explore or facets of Lusitania to rediscover? José Rodrigues Miguéis, in his short story "Viagens na nossa terra" (*Léah*, 1958), has humoristically reduced patriotic national tourism to a comedy of errors through the misadventure-filled travelogue of five *lisboetas* on a day tour of their *pátria bem amada*. His description of the arrival of the tourists at a promontory from which they have their first full view of the sea is given through the words of Artur, the "fifth wheel" of the group:

> E ao fundo o mar. Ah, o MAR! Foi um rito de júbilo dilacerante, que assustou as aves e fez calar os ralos: "O Mar! Lá estai o Mar! Olha o Mar!° Sentimo-nos de repente uma raça marítima; uma espécie de vocação anfíbia até ali então recessiva. E como eu nada dissesse, absorvido, extasiado precisamente na contemplação

From *Hispania*, vol. 74, no. 3 (September 1991). © 1991 by the American Association of Teachers of Spanish and Portuguese.

daquele Mar, a Alzirinha da Fonseca, acotovelando-me nas
costelas com uma espécie de rancor lírico mal disfarçado, muito
próprio da amizade que há muito nos une, perguntou se eu então
não via o Mar, se não me interessava pelo Mar, pela Paisagem,
pela Natureza, "seu mono"! Mas decerto que sim, nem eu faço
outra   coisa,   balbuciei,   despertando   da   minha   quieta
contemplação. Eo Mar perdeu de repente todo o encanto
(Miguéis 73).

It remains for novelist José Saramago (born 1922) to advance the
fictional account of Portuguese voyages to new heights. In his *Memorial do
Convento* (1982) we are carried back to the eighteenth century to witness the
maiden flight of Father Bartolomeu de Gusmão's *passarola*, or primitive
dirigible, "por ares nunca dantes navegados" in 1709. But it is in his *Jangada
de Pedra* (1986) that we accompany the most daring voyage of all, for in this
fanciful novel filled with geopolitical, socio-psychological, and philosophical
implications, the entire Iberian Peninsula breaks loose from Europe and
floats out to sea, with all Portuguese and Spaniards aboard!

Of his *Jangada de Pedra*, author Saramago has said the following in a
December, 1988, interview with the *London Times* "Literary Supplement":

There have been times when this novelist, caught in the mesh of
the fiction he was weaving, began to imagine himself being
transported on that extraordinary stone raft into which he had
transformed the Iberian Peninsula, floating over the Atlantic
Ocean and heading for the South and Utopia. The singular
nature of the allegory was transparent: although preserving some
of the same motives as an ordinary emigrant who departs for
other shores to seek his fortune, there prevailed, in my case, a
definitive and substantial difference, in so far as I took with me in
this unprecedented migration the whole of my native Portugal,
and—without having sought permission from the Spaniards,
therefore without any authority or mandate—Spain itself. Now,
filled by these imaginings of mine, I observed that they brought
no feelings of regret, of melancholy, of distress bordering on
panic or any of the nostalgia summed up by that inevitable
Portuguese word: *saudade*. The reasons will soon become clear.
To all appearances, I was certainly leaving Europe behind for ever
more, but the essential fabric of the immense craft transporting
me continued to nourish the roots of my own identity and of my

collective heritage. I found no reason, therefore, to mourn my
lost treasure. ... I hereby testify that I would be prepared to bring
my wandering raft back from sea after having learned something
during the voyage, if Europe would acknowledge that she is
incomplete without the Iberian Peninsula (*TLS* 1370).

The grand symbol of *A Jangada de Pedra* is that of the journey, whether
by land or sea (since both comprise elements of the novel). The journey is
both that of emigration and of quest, of going *from* and going *to*, and may be
read in a variety of ways in light of the dubious economic benefits which may
or may not accrue to the Iberian Peninsula and the rest of Europe by the
adherence of Spain and Portugal to the European Common Market in the
year 1992. Perhaps absence does in fact make the heart grow fonder, as might
be suggested by the episode in which the youth of all the other European
nations rebel against the *status quo* of their unimaginative cultures and
proclaim in solidarity with the departed countries of Portugal and Spain:
"Nós também somos ibéricos!"

In simultaneous journeys of unification and decentralization, groups
and individuals travel in pursuit of various ends, whether known or unknown;
while the great stone raft on which they ride—the Iberian Peninsula itself—
gently floats out to sea, leaving behind the mass of Europe and, of course, the
Rock of Gibraltar, since that small patch of land pertains to England and
would not be expected to accompany Spain on its voyage! On the grand
overall journey of the *jangada de pedra*, a westerly direction is initially
perceived, bringing general fear to the Azores, which are directly in the path
of the massive stone ship. Fortunately, however, the Peninsula changes
course at a right angle at the last minute and heads toward the general area
of Greenland and Iceland; finally, when the altered latitude is beginning to
show its effect on the climate of the Peninsula and the heads of state of
Canada and the United States ponder how their nations will receive millions
of new Mediterranean immigrants should Portugal and Spain come ashore
on the Atlantic seaboard, another change of route is experienced and the
stone raft eases down the central Atlantic between Africa and South America.
Will it replace the lost Atlantis on future maps of the world? We do not
know.

A lonely seaman in his small sailing craft finds a new lease on life after
the wind fails and he runs out of potable water. On the horizon looms, not a
lifeboat but the entire Iberian Peninsula, and the lone sailor paddles
gratefully into the estuary of the Tagus River in Lisbon, which has come to
rescue him! Between the overarching voyage of the great stone raft and the

microscopic case of this lone sailor, we find the interwoven journeys of a nucleus of five individuals whose paths cross within the national boundaries of Spain and Portugal to form the texture of what may be called the plot of the novel, if indeed there be a plot. But the five individuals in question— three men and two women, including four Portuguese and one Spaniard— have substance not so much because of their personal qualities, well-roundedness or development in the course of the novel (since by all these accounts they fail the test) as because of their symbolism individually and the overarching philosophical and metaphysical implications of their interaction as an evolving unit within a fluid, constantly changing external context. Let us approach each of the five protagonists individually in the order in which they appear in the novel, observing the symbols which distinguish or accompany them and relate them eventually to each other and to the grand scheme of the separation of the Iberian Peninsula from the rest of Europe and its quest for its fluctuating, unknown destiny as a binational block alone on the open sea with an entirely radical "sense of place."

The omniscient third-person narrative voice announces at the beginning of the novel that Joana Carda, residing somewhere in Portugal (presumably the north) has casually scratched a line in the dirt with an elm twig (*uma vara de negrilho*). At the same moment, it would seem, a certain Joaquim Sassa, walking along a beach in northern Portugal, throws a large flat rock into the sea; after skipping once on the surface of the water, it sinks, leaving behind it concentric circles moving progressively outward. A country schoolteacher in central Portugal, José Anaiço, suddenly discovers that an increasingly large flock of starlings seems to be accompanying him wherever he goes. Somewhere near the border of Portugal and Galicia, a certain Maria Guavaira begins to unravel a blue wool sock, winding the wool into a ball. In southern Spain, a pharmacist by the name of Pedro Orce rises from his chair to feel the earth trembling under his feet, while along the Pyrennean border between Spain and France all the dogs have begun to bark even though their breed is normally barkless. As a fine crack develops along the Pyrennees between the two countries, one of the dogs jumps from the French to the Spanish side, where he will continue through the remainder of the book with various names (among them *Ardent* and *Constante*). Joaquim Sassa hears on his transistor radio about Pedro Orce's experience with the trembling earth and sets out in his car, named Dois-Cavalos, to find him, for he calculates that the case occurred precisely when he tossed the stone into the ocean. Along the way south, in Ribatejo, Joaquim crosses paths with José Anaíço and his horde of starlings, and the two travel together to search out Pedro Orce and "compare notes." Once the three have combined forces, they return to Portugal with the intent of traveling together to the north to view the spot where the Peninsula recently separated from Europe, after they join a small wave of tourists viewing the Rock of Gibraltar, now increasingly distant from Spain. All three men are on a kind of summer holiday, and an increasing camaraderie develops among them; naturally, the flock of starlings overhead serves as faithful escort, and cheap luxury hotel rooms are available throughout southern Portugal and Spain since the rich Europeans have all fled back to "Europe" so as not to get caught permanently on the Iberian Peninsula! Once in Lisbon, the three friends are hounded by newspaper reporters and called to give detailed reports to the police of their unique experiences. Soon Joana Carda turns up at the hotel, elm wand in hand, searching for José Anaiço to compare notes on the coincidence of the furrow she had scratched in the soil of northern Portugal (which simply does not disappear) and the appearance of the flock of starlings overhead in Ribatejo. Oddly enough, no sooner has Joana Carda made the acquaintance of José Anaiço than his "guardian angel" starlings wheel as a flock and head south, never to reappear. Joana convinces the "three musketeers" to accompany her to see for themselves that what she has said is true, so off go the four in Dois-Cavalos.

Unlike the tourists of José Rodrigues Miguéis's story, Joana's new friends enjoy a successful trip through Portugal, made even more pleasurable for José Anaiço by a nascent romance with the lady of the *vara de negrilho*. After witnessing the permanent furrow in the earth and trying unsuccessfully to reproduce the phenomenon themselves, all four travelers are startled by the approach of an apparently stray dog with a bit of blue wool hanging from his mouth. His insistence in staying with them convinces them to follow him, driving slowly in Joaquim's car, and old Pedro Orce strikes up an affectionate relationship with the canine guide, who eventually leads them to Maria Guavaira's door. As the unexpected carload of tourists is accommodated by Maria's hospitality, experiences are once again exchanged and plans made to incorporate Maria into the touring group, which is now about to outgrow Dois-Cavalos. Since the car seems about to suffer demise anyway, the five travelers and their dog acquire a sort of covered wagon drawn by one and, eventually, two horses: a new version of Dois-Cavalos! Romance blossoms between Maria Guavaira and Joaquim Sassa as the trip progresses northward to view the point of cleavage between Iberia and Europe, the latter now far distant geographically; the tourists then return south, and both Joana Carda and Maria Guavaira discover they are pregnant. Pedro Orce's health worsens and he dies peacefully, lying on the good earth, which has just ceased to tremble. His faithful canine companion howls briefly, then returns to his customary silence. Plans are made to carry the body back to Pedro's birthplace for burial, and fellow Spaniard Roque Lozano, who with his donkey Platero has crossed paths twice with the tourists, accompanies the cortege to southern Spain. News items received by the group reveal that the Peninsula has just stopped moving and that all the fertile women in Portugal and Spain are pregnant. The friends dig Pedro Orce's grave, and Joana Carda plants her elm wand at his head. ... Perhaps it will bud out next year.

Curiosity is aroused among the five protagonists of *A Jangada de Pedra* by their respective surnames, all uncommon. Joaquim Sassa explains that he has discovered that a *sassa* is a tree of the Nubian desert. Joana Carda's ancestral name was Cardo, but a widowed matriarch's powerful presence resulted in the gender shift generations before Joana's time. José Anaiço's surname is the result of a simple transposition in country speech of an original *Inácio*, while Pedro Orce's reflects his birthplace. Maria Guavaira explains that her name is an original and that it came to her mother in a dream; though this explanation seems to convince her hearers, it may be expected that readers of the novel will link Maria's name literarily with the article of clothing that inspired Portugal's oldest recorded *cantiga de amor*.

> No mundo non me sei parelha,
> mentre me for como me vai,
> ca já moiro por vós—e ai!
> mia senhor branca e vermelha,
> queredes que vos retraia
> quando vos eu vi en saia!
> Mau dia rue levantei,
> que vos enton non vi fea!
>
> E, mia senhor, dês aquel dia', ai!
> me foi a mi mui mal,
> e vós, filha de don Paai
> Moniz, e ben vos semela
> d'haver eu por vós guarvaia,
> pois eu, mia senhor, d'alfaia
> nunca de vós houve nen hei
> valia d'ua correa (Paio Soares de Taveirós, c. 1198).

Maria Guavaira's blue wool thread, unlike Ariadne's, seems to lead the other protagonists into the labyrinth rather than out of it. While Joana Carda forswears any magical powers to her elm wand, noting that it bears no resemblance to the magic wands of folkloric tales, there is an undeniable echo of Aeneas's descent into the underworld which unifies her *vara de negrilho*, José Anaiço's birds, and the Cerberus-like guard dog of many names who comes, after all, from the section of Provence called *Cerbère*. Let us observe Edith Hamilton's paraphrase of the tale:

> Aeneas had been told by the prophet Helenus as soon as he reached the Italian land to seek the cave of the Sybil of Cumae, a woman of deep wisdom, who could foretell the future and would advise him what to do. He found her, and she told him she would guide him to the underworld where he would learn all he needed to know from his father Anchises. ... She warned him, however, that it was no light undertaking. ... First he must find in the forest a golden bough growing on a tree, which he must break off and take with him. Only with this in his hand would he be admitted to hades. ... They went almost hopelessly into the great wilderness of trees where it seemed impossible to find anything. But suddenly they caught sight of two doves, the birds of Venus. The men followed as they flew slowly on until they were close to Lake Avernus. ... Here the doves soared up to a tree through whose foliage came a bright yellow gleam. It was the golden bough. Aeneas plucked it joyfully and took it to the Sibyl. Then, together, prophetess and hero started on their journey. ... Charon was inclined to refuse Aeneas and his guide when they came down to the boat. ... At sight of the golden bough, however, he yielded and took them across. The dog Cerberus was there on the other bank ..., but the Sibyl ... had some cake for him and he gave them no trouble. ... Aeneas soon came upon Anchises, who greeted him with incredulous joy. ... He gave his son instructions how he would best establish his home in Italy and how he could avoid or endure all the hardships that lay before him (Hamilton 226–30).

The bough, the dog, the birds, the boat, and the wise woman who unifies all—are these mere isolated symbols, or could they be part of a grand synchronic scheme? Are they interrelated just as surely as are the ripples to the stone which Joaquim Sassa threw into the ocean? Is there a cause-and-effect linkage between the concentric journeys being realized simultaneously by the Protagonists and by the Peninsula itself, or is all apparent synchronicity pure coincidence? Is every human act a stone in the cosmic ocean which inevitably produces ripples in every other part of the ocean?

These are the fundamental issues raised by *A Jangada de Pedra*, and to them we now turn our attention.

The initial chapter of the novel presents as simultaneous at least five of the scattered events recorded: the furrowing of the soil by Joana Carda, the barking of the hitherto barkless dogs, the hurling of the stone into the ocean by Joaquim Sassa, the splitting of the Pyrennees, and the seismographic sensations of Pedro Orce. The remaining two "events" or processes—the appearance of the flock of starlings over José Anaiço and the unraveling of the blue woolen sock by Maria Guavaira—are assumed to have their onset within a few minutes or hours of the preceding group. The novel's first word—*Quando*—sets the tone for the underlying assumption of synchronicity which pervades the novel:

> Quando Joana Carda' riscou o chão com a vara de negrilho, todos
> os cães de Cerbère começaram a ladrar, lançando em pânico e terror
> os habitantes, pois desde os tempos mais antigos se acreditava que,
> ladrando ali animais caninos que sempre tinham sido mudos, estaria
> o mundo universal próximo de extinguir-se (Saramago 9).

Throughout the remainder of the work the leitmotivs of stone, elm wand, blue thread, dog, starlings, and trembling earth recur alone and in concert as in a musical composition. Of the 330 pages of the novel, the dog appears in 90, the stone in slightly over 50, the starlings in 45, the elm wand in 35 and the references to trembling earth and blue thread in 20 each.

Is apparent synchronicity fortuitous, or is there a covert relation of cause-and-effect in such cases? If the latter be true, which of the actions precipitated the others, and in what order? Was the earth trembling before Pedro Orce rose from his chair and put his feet on the floor? Did Joaquim Sassa's throwing of the stone in some way cause the Pyrennees to split, or was it perhaps Joana Carda's furrowing of the earth with her twig that produced the slight perturbation that upset the mountain chain? Hypotheses crowd the pages of the novel, which is in its way a fictional essay on this and related philosophical subjects. Let us hear the novel's own words in a selection of textual quotations arranged in simple order of appearance:

> Todas estas coisas, mesmo quando o não parecerem, estão ligadas
> entre si (Saramago 19).

> Não há um só destino, ao contrário do que tínhamos aprendido
> nos fados e canções. Ninguém foge ao seu destino, pode sempre

acontecer que nos venha a calhar, subitamente, o destino doutra pessoa (Saramago 116).

Ainda há quem não acredite em coincidências, quando coincidências é o que mais se encontra e prepara no mundo, se não são as coincidências a própria lógica do mundo (Saramago 127).

O que tem de ser, tem de ser, e tem muita força, não se pode resistir-lhe. ... A vida está cheia de pequenos acontecimentos que parecem ter pouca importância, outros há que num certo momento ocuparam a atenção toda, e quando mais tarde, à luz das suas consequências, os reapreciarnos, vê-se que destes esmoreceu a lembrança, ao passo que aqueles ganharam título de facto decisivo ou, pelo menos, malha de ligação duma cadeia sucessiva e significativa de eventos (Saramago 141).

Não é da vara, não é da pessoa, foi do momento, o momento é que conta. ... A sua vara, a pedra de Joaquim Sassa, os estorninhos de José Anaiço, serviram uma vez, nãoservirão mais. São como os homens e as mulheres, que também só uma vez servem (Saramago 149).

O instinto conduz este cão, mas não sabemos o quê ou quem conduz o instinto, e se um destes dias tivermos do estranho caso apresentado uma primeira explicação, o mais provável é que tal explicação não passe de aprência dela, excepto se da explicação pudermos ter uma explicação e assim sucessivamente, até áquele derradeiro instante em que não haveria nada para explicar o montante do explicado, daí para trás supomos que será o reino do caos (Saramago 180).

Embora pareça absurdo, acabámos por acreditar que existe uma relação qualquer entre o que nos aconteceu e a separação de Espanha e Portugal da Europa (Saramago 189).

Nós aqui vamos andando sobre a península, a península navega sobre o mar, o mar roda com a terra a que pertence, e a terra vai rodando sobre si mesma, e, enquanto roda sobre si mesma, roda também à volta do sol, e o sol também gira sobre si mesmo, e tudo isto junto vai na direcção da tal constelação, então o que eu pergunto, se não somos o extremo menor desta cadeia de movimentos dentro de movimentos, o que eu gostaria de saber é o que é que se move dentro de nós e para onde vai ... que nome finalmente tem o que a tudo move, de uma extremidade da cadeia à outra, ou cadeia não existirá e o universo talvez seja um anel, simultaneamente tão delgado que parece que só nós, e o que em nós cabe, cabemos nele, e tão grosso que possa conter a máxima dimensão do universo que ele prório é (Saramago 269).

Meu Deus, meu Deus, como todas as coisas deste mundo estão entre si ligadas, e nós a julgar que cortamos ou atamos quando queremos, por nossa única vontade, esse é o maior dos erros, e tantas lições nos têm sido dadas em contrário, um risco no chão, um bando de estorninhos, uma pedina atirada ao mar, um pé-de-meia de lã azul, se a cegos mostramos, se a gente endurecida e surda pregoamos (Saramago 328).

The consensus of these probing quotations supports what might be called paradoxically the "synchronicity of intentional coincidences." Rather than a linear sequence of cause-and-effect, there is perceived throughout the universe a meaningful and concentric overlapping and interpenetration of lives and events at all levels. Each human act is therefore potentially significant in a cosmic sense even when it appears to be merely a random occurrence.

The echoing of Camões's *Lusíadas* (Canto X) in the last of these quotations, appearing two pages from the end of the novel, leads us to the quintessentially Portuguese nature of the conscience of several of the protagonists and of the work itself. Against the argument that the *moment* or *fate* has produced the synchronicity of the several phenomena experienced by Joana Carda, Joaquim Sassa, José Anaiço, Pedro Orce and Maria Guavaira appears what Alexandre O'Neill has called the "cosmic guilt" complex of the Lusitanian nation. Joana Carda and Joaquim Sassa both feel individually responsible for the separation of the Peninsula from the rest of Europe; note the following dialog between the latter and José:

Quem sabe se a culpa não é minha, murmurou Joaquim Sassa. No te ponhas em conta tão alta, ao ponto de te considerares culpado de tudo. ... Atirei uma pedra ao mar e há quem acredite que foi razão de arrancar-se a península à Europa. Se um dia tiveres um filho, ele morrerá porque tu nasceste, desse crime ninguém te absolverá, as mãos que fazem e tecem são as mesmas que desfazem e destecem, o certo gera o errado, o errado produz o certo. Fraca consolação para um aflito. Não há consolação, amigo triste, o homem é um animal inconsolável (Saramago 73).

By virtue of the equalization of opposites just observed by José Anaiço, however, and in harmony with the timeless maritime destiny of the Portuguese, it is the venturing of the Peninsula into the primordial waters that cover the earth that symbolizes potential rebirth and cosmic baptism so that a better human race may face a better future. Pondering the collective pregnancy of all the fertile women of Spain and Portugal, the omniscient third person narrative voice tells us:

Há por cima de nós um lume vivo, assim como se o homem, afinal, não tivesse de sair com históricos vagares da animalidade e pudesse ser posto outra vez, inteiro e lúcido, num mundo novamente formado, limpo e de beleza intacta. Tendo tudo isto acontecido, dizendo o tal português poeta que a península é uma criança que viajando se formou e agora se revolve no mar para nascer, como se estivesse no interior de um útero aquático, que motivos haveria para espantar-nos de que os humanos úteros das mulheres ocupassem, acaso as fecundou a grande pedra que desce para o sul, sabemos nós lá se são malmente filhas dos homens estas novas crianças, ou se é seu pai o gigantesco talha-mar que vai empurrando as ondas à sua frente, penetrando-as, águas murmurantes, o sopro e o suspiro dos ventos (Saramago 319).

From the abstract level of Thomistic argumentation of first causes or prime movers through the pragmatic consideration of national consciousness and international relations in a changing world, we come at last to an inherently textual problem: how to present synchronicity on the printed page and what to expect of the synchronicity of a "readerly" text. Again, music serves as the ideal vehicle for synchronic communication, in the narrator's opinion, especially the operatic genre:

Dificílimo acto é o de escrever, responsabilidade das maiores, basta pensar no extenuante trabalho que será dispor por ordem temporal os acontecimentos, primeiro este, depois aquele, ou, se tal mais convém às necessidades do efeito, o sucesso de hoje posto antes do episódio de ontem e outras não menos arriscadas acrobacias, o passado como se tivesse sido agora, o presente como o contínuo sem presente nem fim, mas por muito que se esforcem os autores, uma habilidade não podem cometer, pôr por escrito, no mesmo tempo, dois casos no mesmo tempo acontecidos. Há quem julgue que a dificuldade fica resolvida dividindo a página em duas colunas, lado a lado, mas o ardil é ingénuo, porque primeiro se escreveu uma e só depois a outra, sem esquecer que o leitor terá de ler primeiro esta e depois aquela, ou vice-versa, quem está bem são os cantores de ópera, cada um com a sua parte nos concertantes, três quatro cinco seis entre tenores baixos sopranos e barítonos, todos a cantar palavras diferentes, por exemplo, o cínico escarnecendo, a ingénua suplicando, o galã tardo em acudir, ao espectador o que lhe interessa é a música, já o leitor não é assim, quer tudo explicado, sílaba por sílaba e uma após outra, cano aqui se mostram (Saramago 14).

Para que as coisas existam duas condições são necessárias, que homem as veja e homem lhes ponha nome (Saramago 71).

Estes lugares são de meter medo. ... Em Venta Micena é bem pior, foi lá que eu nasci, ambiguidade formal que tanto significa o que parece como o seu exacto contrário, dependendo mais do leitor do que da leitura, embora esta em tudo dependa daquele, por isso nos é tão difícil saber quem lê o que foi lido e como ficou o que foi lido por quem leu (Saramago 83).

In *A Jangada de Pedra*'s layering of concentric journeys are embedded concentric levels of symbolism and synchronicity which lure the reader back repeatedly to the quest of the text. As the narrator says:

Uma palavra, quando dita, dura mais que o som e os sons que a formaram, fica por aí, invisível e inaudível para poder guardar o seu próprio segredo, uma espécie de semente oculta debaixo da terra, que germina longe dos olhos, até que de repente afasta o torrão e aparece à luz, um talo enrolado, uma folha amarrotada que lentamente se desdobra (Saramago 286).

We may say of this text, with appropriately polysemic connotation and in the words and spirit of José Saramago himself: "O conteúdo pôde ser maior que o continente" (Saramago 18). The Iberian Peninsula, by virtue of its fortuitous separation from the rest of Europe, becomes a new continent in its own right, with the potentially signified looming ever more significant than the signifier itself. Of the five human protagonists of the terrestrial quest within the maritime journey, the three males represent three fields of professional training: Joaquim Sassa is an engineer, José Anaiço a teacher, and Pedro Orce a pharmacist. All three, however, follow the course set for them by the three "non-professionals": Joana Carda with her wand of elm, Maria Guavaira with her horsedrawn carriage, and the ubiquitous "dog for all seasons." Even the mechanical "Dois-Cavalos" succumbs to a literally horse-powered vehicle! As throughout the history of Portugal in its national and international affairs, the "scientific" or "analytical" of the head gives place to the intuitive and spontaneous of the heart. The women form the firm foundation of insight and orientation within the constantly evolving external world, and it is they who bear the symbols of promise for a brighter future of continued life on the new continent: their pregnant wombs and the ever-green *vara de negrilho*, with which they bless even the tomb of the defunct Pedro Orce.

There runs throughout *A Jangada de Pedra*, alongside its gentle irony regarding the foibles of human and nationalistic nature in the areas of communication and international understanding, an optimistic and robust vein of confidence in the future. To the degree that the institutional powers-that-be and the status quo are subverted by the latent powers of nature, the horizon is cleared for a simpler, more instinctive and humanitarian impulse to surge forth. Symbolically, it is Portugal, ever looking outward to new challenges as in centuries of yore, who leads the way through "azares nunca dantes navegados" and models a nucleus of unprejudiced solidarity and mutual understanding to the rest of the world.

WORKS CITED

Frazer, Sir James George. *The New Golden Bough*. New York: Anchor Books, 1961.
Hamilton, Edith. *Mythology*. New York: Mentor Books, 1942.
Lopes, Oscar. *Os sinais e os sentidos*. Lisbon: Editorial Caminho, 1986.
Miguéis, José Rodrigues. *Léah*. Lisbon: Estúdios Cor, 1958.
Saramago, José. *A Jangada de Pedra*. Lisbon: Editorial Caminho, 1986.
Seixo, Maria Alzira. *O essencial sobre José Saramago*. Lisbon: Imprensa Nacional/Casa da Moeda, 1987.
Times Literary Supplement (Dec. 9–15, 1988). London.

GENE STEVEN FORREST

The Dialectics of History in Two Dramas of José Saramago

Contemporary theories regarding historiography remind us that all representations of history—including those of the so-called objective or proto-scientific stance—are implicitly "metahistorical" in that they entail a preliminary selection of formal or narrative strategies which ultimately reveal one ideological bias or another.[1] The historical text, therefore, is also a literary or fictive creation, although the reverse is also true that the literary work is never far removed from history. Consequently, the historian's claims to empirical veracity and the poet's pursuit of esthetic "purity" are equally illusive. José Saramago, in his novels and dramatic works, eschews both notions and openly subverts the concept of an official, incontrovertible record of the past at the same time that he employs history as a metaphor for his own subjective vision of society, specifically—though not exclusively—that of his native Portugal. In the two dramas that I will be discussing, *A noite* (1979) and *Que farei com este livro?* (1980), historical representation, rather than connoting a static representation of events, is essentially a vital dialectic or reassessment of the Portuguese past with reference to the present and the future.[2]

Central to the thematic focus and dramatic tension of both plays is the historical text itself, its creation, publication and public reception or interpretation. *A noite*, set entirely in the editing room of a Lisbon newspaper

From *Hispanófila*, vol. 106 (September 1992). © 1992 by *Hispanófila*.

on the fateful evening of April 24, 1974, portrays the struggle of a small
faction of the journal's staff to print a full and accurate account of the military
coup which was to bring an end to "Salazarism" and the regime of Marcello
Caetano. *Que farei com este livro?*, written, no doubt, in commemoration of
the three-hundredth anniversary of Camões's death, traces the difficult
circumstances surrounding the publication of *Os Lusíadas* in 1572. Despite
the obvious formalistic differences which would appear to separate both
texts, in Saramago's demythologization of the historical record, the so-called
objective journalistic chronicle and the poetic account are shown to be
basically subjective narratives which consist of a partial and—in some
instances—intentionally falsified rendering of factual events. As a result of
this reductive process, the fine line separating fact and fiction is erased and
conventionally-held assumptions regarding the past are challenged and
repudiated.

To begin with, Saramago places both texts within the crucible of social,
political and economic forces which exert an oppressively deterministic
influence over their final publication. Thus, both texts are shaped by a series
of vested interests, hidden agendas and conventions which, as is often the
case, work at cross-purposes with the texts' avowed objectives. Most
apparent among such obtrusive forces is official censorship, the daily
inspection and "cuts" imposed by the military authorities and foreign
governments on the press in *A noite* and obligatory courtly favor and
inquisitorial review to which *Os Lusíadas* is subjected in *Que farei*. No less
formidable in molding both texts are the financial interests which further
compromise the works' independence and belie any pretense of objectivity or
professional integrity. Pointing to such blatant manipulation of the press,
Manuel Torres, the leading voice of dissent on the newspaper, exclaims: "A
informação não é objectiva, e quanto a neutralidade, é tão neutral como a
Suíça. ... O dono do dinheiro é sempre o dono do poder, mesmo quando não
aparece na primeira fila como tal. Quem tem o poder, tem a informação que
defenderá os interesses do dinheiro que esse poder serve" / "News is not
objective, and as for neutrality, it's as neutral as Switzerland. ... He who
possesses money is always the master of power even when he doesn't appear
up front as such. He who possesses power, possesses the news which will
defend the financial interests which serve that power" (57–58).[3] Such
economic concerns oblige the indigent Luís de Camões to court favor under
the most humiliating of circumstances, and his poem's glowing dedication to
the young monarch, Dom Sebastião—a panegyric replete with unintentional
irony in light of impending events—is prompted more by economic necessity
than deeply-felt patriotism.

An end result of the powerful intrusion of external interests into the text is the virtual proscription of the masses of nameless peasants and workers from the conventional historical record. Such glaring lapses or deletions— which Saramago's novels in large measure attempt to redress—[4] provide the basis for one of the Portuguese writer's most telling indictments of traditional historiography. In *A noite*, for instance, Manuel Torres is punished for his liberal views by being relegated to the provincial news desk, presumably because such news is considered less significant or, in other words, "marketable" than other items. It is his story which is unquestionably deleted to make room for a vacuous editorial submitted at the last minute by the editor and chief. This same theme reappears in *Que farei* when Camões's friend, the historian Diogo de Couto, suggests that the poet incorporate into *Os Lusíadas* a description of the plague which was decimating Lisbon at that time. Camões is quite taken aback by the idea that the suffering of the ordinary populace might be a fitting subject for his epic poem, and he can only respond: "Estranha idea esa ... Não se usa" / "That's a strange notion ... It's not customary" (59).

In addition to calling attention to the distortion of the historical text through the arbitrary focussing of the historical field, Saramago addresses the basic unreliability of language itself as an objective vehicle for recording facts. This is particularly true in the case of *A noite* where language, rather than elucidating meaning, serves to obscure it. An editorial attack on intellectuals and the Left—transcribed by Saramago from the Fascist journal *Época* of April, 1973—is written in such a turbid and imprecise style as to render its thesis nearly incomprehensible. This is intentionally so, for, as its author explains, despite his anti-progressive stance, expediency demands that he express his ideas with a prudent and opportune neutrality: "Politicamente, é um erro queimar pontes que não temos a certeza de não precisar de vir a passar" / "Politically, it's a mistake to burn bridges which one is not certain not to have to cross some day" (39). Playing it safe and keeping one's options as flexible as possible require a journalistic jargon which is appropriately noncommittal and devoid of meaning. Language serves a similar purpose in *Que farei* to the extent that the indigent Camões is obliged to win the favor of noble and cleric alike through the intricate arguments and conceits which he must wield with utmost skill. But more importantly, as poetry, language serves a purpose far beyond that of literal discourse since language, through the ludic artifice of trope and rhyme, achieves a polysemy which is the essence of its creative objective.

Assuming even that language may be employed unambiguously in conveying the most transparent meaning, there is no guarantee that such language will be accurately received or understood. The historical text—or any text for that matter—is not fixed or absolute but, in reality, is entirely relative or constantly changing in accordance with successive readings.[5] This is a fact which the protagonist of *Que farei* must come to realize and use to his own advantage. Once he has terminated his manuscript, Camões is self-confident that it will be well received, and he naively assumes that his poem is complete. In the course of the play, however, he realizes that *his* work, if it is to enter the public domain, must become a *collective* work, beholden to some for financial and political sponsorship, dependent on others for review and subsequent addenda and deletions. In the final analysis, the work that emerges will reflect the reading which prevails: "a parte que ficar vencedora fará que seja o livro lido com os olhos que mais the convierem" / "the party which triumphs will make sure that the book is read in such a way that serves its best interests" (106). Moreover, when Camões is forced to relinquish his copyright in order to publish the opus, he quite literally loses any control over his creation. The double interrogative posed by Camões at the play's conclusion: "Que farei com este livro? ... Que fareis com este livro?" / "What will I do with this book? ... What will you do with this book?" (174), alludes to the multiplicity of future readings which conclusively alienate the author from his text.

Having touched on the fundamental bases for Saramago's deconstruction of the historical text, I will turn my attention to the Portuguese writer's specific repudiation of the myths enshrouding his own nation's past. In *A noite* and *Que farei com este livro?*, Saramago undermines myth by constructing both plays along an antagonistic or ironic axis of binary opposition. This ironic or satirical "emplotment"[6] is the playwright's key structural strategy for underscoring the disparity between the official or epic record of events and a differing, unofficial representation of these same events. In consonance with this self-conscious juxtaposition of mutually exclusive opposites, metaphor is the principal stylistic device for achieving the skeptical, dialectical approach to the past.

The contrast of night and dawn (darkness and light) which corresponds to *A noite*'s temporal and dramatic evolution from the first to the second act, clearly denotes the ignorance and lethargy of the newsroom and all that it represents and, on the other hand, the enlightended struggle for change which is taking place in the streets. Equally significant as the night/dawn paradigm is the polarization of horizontal and vertical planes; the former, representing the oppressive chain of command from inner executive chambers to outer newsroom, and the latter, denoting a radical overturning of the existing power structure. As is so often the case in Saramago's novels, horizontality and verticality connote, respectively, submission to power and liberation from power.[7] This is manifest in the kinetic symbolism suggested by the following stage directions: "Nota-se uma nítida, embora acentuada, mostra de dependência do Director em relação ao Visitante" / "One can see a clear, although accentuated, sign of dependency on the part of the Director in relation to the Visitor" (16); "Rafael entra na Redacção. A subservencia diminui" / "Rafael enters the Copyroom. His subservience diminishes" (17). More explicitly, horizontality is synonymous with stultifying and inflexible routine to which the idealistic aspirations of Torres are in sharp contrast. The following quote in which Torres encourages a young apprentice journalist is particularly significant in this regard: "pobre de ti se não conservares a verticalidade que tens hoje. E não to deixes prender por admirações. ... A nossa vida é uma contínua resistencia a franqueza, à renúncia, ao conformismo ..." / "poor you if you don't maintain the verticality which you have today. And don't be taken in by admiration. ... Our existence is a constant struggle with candor, with rejection, with conformity ..." (65). At the play's conclusion, this verticality succeeds in displacing horizontality through two acts of insubordination which transgress the stratified, established order. In the context of the newspaper, the typesetters enter the editorial room and demand that the newspaper print a truthful account of events, and, in the national arena, political upheaval—likened by the journal's Editor to a series of seismic jolts (19)—shatters the status quo with the force of a devastating earthquake.

In terms of language, horizontality bespeaks the uninspired jargon of convention which through routine and deceptive manipulation becomes atrophied and meaningless. Even Torres finds himself the unwitting perpetrator of such fossilized discourse when, during a conversation with his superior, Valadares, he utters: "Estou ao seu dispor" / "I'm at your disposal" (46), a phrase he subsequently disavows: "É uma daqueles trastes que herdámos dos antepasados, sem saber como nem de quem, uma frase que não significa nada. E uma pequena hipocresia" / "It's one of those old pieces of junk which we inherited from our ancestors, without knowing how or from whom, a sentence which means nothing. It's a minor hypocrisy" (47). Perhaps Torres's definitive rejection of such language—and Saramago's most ironic reassessment of the notion of so-called journalistic integrity and devotion to truth—is his observation that the newspaper's supreme and most fitting purpose was in lining the garbage dispensers of the Lisbon populace, "Porque tudo aquilo era lixo" / "Because all that was garbage" (56).

Following this identical strategy of ironic juxtaposition, in his subsequent play, Saramago sets Camões and his epic vision of Portuguese conquest and exploration within the broader framework of the political and social climate of late sixteenth-century Portugal. The alarming disparity which exists between Camões's glorious account of Portuguese achievement and the entirely antiheroic state of things he finds upon his return to Lisbon in 1570 is developed throughout *Que farei* by means of a series of metaphorical motifs. Perhaps the most obvious of these is the foreboding and noxious fog which hangs over the land and which alludes to the inexperienced and irresponsible young king, Dom Sebastião, who, it becomes immediately apparent from the first scene, is the pawn of ambitious advisors and the object of intense political intrigue. Engulfed in such fog, the "ship of state" is, as one character suggests, a ship without rudder or mast ("este barco sem leme nem mastro" [61]) and, consequently, faces a precarious future and nearly certain destruction. This image, naturally, flies in the face of the achievements of former monarchs and the navigational prowess of men such as Vasco da Gama to whom Camões devotes his epic work.

Concealed beneath this same dense mist are disturbing questions raised in the play's opening scene concerning the young monarch's interest in marriage and even his virility. Beyond the supremely important matter of the succession and national stability and sovereignty which such questions address, Sebastião's alleged impotency cast his intense religiosity and all-consuming passion for foreign conquest in an almost perverse or abnormal light. This certainly is Diogo do Couto's implication when he describes the king in the following terms: "Gosta de caçar e montear, arrenega do governo do reino, reza mais do que a rei convém. Mas é corajoso. Diz-se que só tem medo de uma coisa, do casamento. ... este rei não basta sequer para Portugal, como pode chegar para tão grande sonho de conquista?" / "He enjoys hunting and riding, neglects the administration of the realm and prays more than is fitting for a king. But he is brave. It is said that he fears only one thing: marriage. ... this king is hardly sufficient for Portugal, how can he measure up to such an ambitious dream of conquest?" (62). Indeed, nothing could be further from Camões's description of da Gama and his robust and virile crew on Venus's Isle of Love in Canto Nine of *Os Lusíadas*, nor, for that matter, the flattering portrait and glowing prophesies of future conquest, both military and amorous, contained in the dedication to Sebastião in Canto One of that same work.

Further symptomatic of this demythologization of Portuguese militarism, imperialism and missionary zeal is Saramago's treatment of the plague which ravaged Lisbon in 1570. Although a well-documented event, the plague is fully exploited artistically in order to create a symbol of transcendent meaning. For one thing, the plague is responsible for the play's split dramatic setting between the royal court at Almeirim and Lisbon, for in their haste to escape the congestion and risk of contagion in the port city, the privileged few have taken up residence outside the capital. Lacking the resources to do so, Camões, his mother and those like them must face the odds of survival in the narrow and crowded dwellings of the Mouraria. The *peste*, in other words, focusses attention on the radical separation of the classes and the disproportionate suffering of the masses. For another thing, the Lisbon plague provides an appropriate introduction to the malaise which Camões and his companion, Diogo do Couto, suffer as the result of their years of trial and misfortune in India. India, in fact, despite the wealth and glory that it has brought to a fortunate minority, is perceived as a terrible liability or "illness" which has been inflicted on the Portuguese people. "A India será," says Diogo do Couto, "ou cuido que já o é, uma doença de Portugal. Queira Deus que não mortal doença." / "India will be, or I believe it already is, a malady of Portugal. I pray not a fatal malady" (49). In the course of the play, do Couto comes to see that India is but a symptom of a widespread national affliction whose origin is to be found in the Portuguese fixation with imperial conquest and religious indoctrination. Dom Sebastião and the plague, then, are the outcome of an official ethos carried to excess, and, in the end, do Couto returns to India having reached the conclusion that "Portugal morre de tristeza" / "Portugal is dying of sadness" (135).

Do Couto's disillusionment with the motherland reflects the level of intolerance and injustice he witnesses there. This issue of justice constitutes a third essential motif which Saramago employs in order to invalidate further the official, patriotic myths. Camões's epic vision of a Ptolemaic universe of harmonious concentric spheres, ruled by one divine lawgiver and judge (Canto Ten of *Os Lusíadas*), is offset by his own harsh discovery of disorder and injustice at home in Portugal. Rather than obeying any objective or systematic standard or procedure, the official channels of review and appeal depend wholly upon self-interest and intrigue. As the perceptive historian and humanist Damião de Góis observes, only the intercession of highly placed persons at Court and in the Inquisition can tip the scales of justice in Camões's favor: "A vossa obra será publicada, Luís Vaz, mas só quando, claramente, a balança pender para um lado ou para outro." / "Your work will be published, Luís Vaz, but only when, clearly, the scales tip to one side or another" (105). Ironically, these same capricious scales are weighed against de Góis, and he is secretly denounced and encarcerated by the Holy Office. When Camões inquires about the fate of the venerable old scholar, he is reprimanded and told that such concern may jeopardize the publication of *Os*

Lusíadas as well as place its author under suspicion of heretical misconduct. Although Camões ultimately is successful in passing the Inquisitorial review process, he only does so at a terrible cost to his own conscience and faith in justice.

Saramago deals his final and perhaps supreme blow in subverting the heroic paradigm at the conclusion of both plays where, rather than a glorious apotheosis or epic prophecy, dramatic "closure" is unresolved, and the protagonist is relegated to a place of decentralized or peripheral uncertainty (Lutwack 43). This strategy is quintessentially dialectical in that it obliges the viewer to reach his or her own conclusions on the basis of information not provided for in the play. Camões's inquiry "Que fareis com este livro?" implicitly alludes to all of the potential readings and misreadings of his work and, by extension, to the ultranationalistic and colonialist propaganda for which author and text were to become the unwitting collaborators and hallmarks.[8] Implicit as well in Camões's inquiry is the tragic fate of Dom Sebastião and its disastrous implications for Portuguese expansionism and sovereignty. Similarly, the unresolved confrontation between reactionary, neutral and radical members of the newspaper staff and their respective hypotheses concerning the outcome of Saraiva de Carvalho's uprising must elicit the knowing response of an audience only too familiar with the turbulent aftermath of that auspicious event.

Insofar as Saramago's dialectical representation of Portuguese history entails an unrelenting destruction of commonly held assumptions regarding the past through satire and parody, it would appear that his basic outlook on history is one of skepticism and profound pessimism. Indeed, in a recent interview, the Portuguese writer expresses little hope for humanity's ability to overcome its demons and defines man as a "cosmic mistake" (Guardiola 4). Despite such negativism, however, Saramago's deconstruction of official, written history is accompanied by a vindication of silent, unwritten history which reflects his abiding struggle on behalf of social justice and truth. By casting his spotlight on the so-called marginal areas of society, Saramago not only inverts and, thus, subverts the conventional order of things, but, in a more constructive sense, "resurrects" from oblivion the masses of men and women traditionally denied a voice in the historical chronicle.[9] This is particularly true in the case of the latter group, and in both *A noite* and *Que farei*, women—specifically and respectively, the apprentice reporter, Claudia, and Camões's mother and his former lover and friend, Francisca de Aragão— play pivotal roles both in the dramatic denouement and in the documentation of historical events.

As is often the case in Saramago's works, the questioning of conventional artistic canons leads inevitably to a reevaluation of society, its institutions and ethos (Ribelo 31–32). Thus, the drafting and publication of two historical texts, the one, a journalistic chronicle, and the other, an epic poem, give rise to a reassessment of society itself. Why, Saramago's protagonists ask over and over again, should the interests of the very few, by sheer dint of their political and economic power, so totally outweigh those of the predominant majority, and why should those of vision and conscience who attempt to challenge or subvert such injustice meet with official opposition and censure? Although Saramago himself proffers no answers to such questions nor any doctrinaire blueprint for change,[10] the "open," unresolved finale of both dramatic works tacitly begs the audience's collaboration in seeking some future solution. Much like Camões and the divided newspaper staff, Saramago must leave his own version of history to the uncertain readings and interpretations of future generations. As Portugal's most widely translated and read contemporary writer (Losada 3), however, Saramago is, at least, assured that his version of history will be judged and debated by a large and increasingly international audience for a long time to come.

NOTES

1. Of particular relevance to this discussion are the following works: Roland Barthes, "The Discourse of History" (1981) and Hayden White, *The Content of Form: Narrative Discourse and Historical Representation* (1987).

2. Luiz Francisco Rebello likens such theater to the Brechtian epic model to which he also ascribes other well-known Portuguese works such as Bernardo Santareno's *O Judeo* and José Cardoso Pires' *O render dos heróis* (10–11).

3. All English translations from the Portuguese are my own.

4. See Silva 28 and Bértolo 4.

5. Affirming the relativity of all texts, Saramago has stated that "A partir del momento en que se admite que el libro es intocable, que el libro tiene razón para siempre, el pensamiento se paraliza ..." / "Once one accepts that a book is untouchable, that a book is correct for all time, thought becomes paralized ..." (Guardiola 4).

6. White uses this term to denote narrative structure (*Metahistory* 8).

7. See Silva 239 and Ribelo 33.

8. Eduardo Lourenço, alluding to this political exploitation of Camões and the anti-nationalistic backlash of democratic, liberal sentiment which characterized Saramago and other writers in the wake of April 1974, writes: "Houve, portanto, algumas tentativas de contrariar a imagen militante, a epopeia ao mesmo tempo imperial e vagamente guerreira que é simbolizada n'*Os Lusíadas*, por uma outra forma de ver o nosso próprio destino ..." / "There were, therefore, attempts, to contradict the militant image, the imperial and at the same time vaguely warlike epic symbolized in *Os Lusíadas*, with another means for viewing our own destiny ..." (31).

9. See Silva 266, Losada 3 and Ribelo 33.

10. Saramago has denied any partisan bias in his writings, and, in reference to *A noite*, states: "Não gosto de ... demagogia. ... Mesmo cuando escrevi textos ficcionais com maior vinculação com os fatos políticos, como *A noite*, não passei pela tentação de demagogia e nem a crítica de extrema-direita pode apontar ou ousar falar de qualquer forma de demagogia. Escrevo os livros que entendo. A competição do escritor é pessoal e não partidária" / "I don't care for ... demogoguery. ... Even when I wrote fictional texts which were more closely related to political facts, like *A noite*, I was not tempted by demogoguery, and not even the criticism of the extreme right could point out or dare speak of any form of demogoguery. I write my own books. The writer's debate is personal and not partisan" (in Medina 267).

WORKS CITED

Barthes, Roland. "The Discourse of History." Trans. Stephen Bann. *Comparative Criticism: A Yearbook*. Ed. E.S. Shaffer. Vol. 3. Cambridge: Cambridge Univ. Press, 1981.

Bértolo, Constantino. "Alfa y omega de Saramago." Rev of *Manual de pintura y caligrafia* and *Historia do cerco de Lisboa*, by José Saramago. Literary supplement of Intl. ed. *El Pais* 4 Sept. 1989: 4–5.

Guardiola, Nicole. "Como náufrago a la deriva." Literary supplement of intl. ed. *El País* 7 May 1990: 4.

Losada, Basilio. "Una voz ibérica." Literary supplement of intl. ed. *El Pais* 5 March 1990: 3.

Lourenço, Eduardo. "Da contra-epopéia a não epopéia: de Fernão Mendes Pinto a Ricardo Reis." *Revista Crítica de Ciencias Sociais* 18/19/20 (1986): 27–35.

Lutwack, Leonard. *The Role of Place in Literature*. Syracuse: Syracuse Univ. Press, 1984.

Medina, Cremilda de Araújo. *Viagem à literatura portuguesa contemporânea*. Rio de Janeiro: Nórdica, 1983.

Rebello, Luiz Francisco. Preface. *Que farei com este livro?* By José Saramago. Lisbon: Editorial Caminho, 1988.

Ribelo, Luis de Sousa. Preface. *Manual de pintura e caligrafia*. By José Saramago. 3rd. ed. Lisbon: Editorial Caminho, 1985.

Saramago, José. *A noite*. 2nd. ed. Lisbon: Editorial Caminho, 1987.

———. *Que farei com este livro?* Lisbon: Editorial Caminho, 1988.

Silva, Teresa Cristina Cerdeira da. *José Saramago entre a historia e a ficção: uma saga de portugueses*. Lisbon: Publicações Dom Quixote, 1989.

White, Hayden. *Metahistory: The Historical Imagination in Nineteenth-Century Europe*. Baltimore: The Johns Hopkins Univ. Press, 1973.

———. *The Content of the Form: Narrative Discourse and Historical Representation*. Baltimore: The Johns Hopkins Univ. Press, 1987.

GIOVANNI PONTIERO

José Saramago and O Ano da Morte de Ricardo Reis (The Year of the Death of Ricardo Reis): *The Making of a Masterpiece*

As the title suggests, this fourth novel by José Saramago is dominated by the presence of Ricardo Reis, one of the heteronyms of the poet Fernando Pessoa (1888–1935), Portugal's most famous poet since Camoens. Pessoa insisted that his three main heteronyms (Alvaro de Campos, Alberto Caeiro and Ricardo Reis) were not mere pseudonyms but evidence of the multiple personalities we all possess and contrasting facets of our innumerable selves. Saramago ingeniously probes the relationship between Pessoa and Reis further, by allowing the heteronym to outlive his creator by nine months, while summoning Pessoa from his tomb to renew friendship with Reis, who has just returned to Portugal after sixteen years of exile in Brazil.

Reis' return to Portugal can be seen as a quest, a pilgrimage to his creator's grave, a return to his spiritual roots, spurred on by the need to renew an unfinished dialogue about life and art, reality and illusion. Both Pessoa and Reis are haunted by unresolved enigmas and the poet confides: '... morri antes de ter percebido se é o poeta que se finge de homem ou o homem que se finge de poeta'.[1]

The Lisbon Reis encounters on his return is a sombre and silent city, its topography a labyrinth of reminiscences. A constant drizzle and darkness emphasize the all-pervading sense of alienation and the author suggests that what Reis needs is

From *Bulletin of Hispanic Studies*, vol. 71, no. 1 (January 1994). © 1994 Liverpool University Press.

um cãozito de cego, uma bengalita, uma luz adiante, que este
mundo e esta Lisboa são uma névoa escura onde se perde o sul e
o norte, o leste e o oeste, onde o único caminho aberto é para
baixo ... (91)

The Lisbon depicted by Saramago is unmistakably that of the mid-
1930s. The reader has the impression of scanning photographs of the period,
the city's monuments and statues reminding us of Portugal's former glory,
once a great sea-faring nation and mighty empire, but now much diminished.
In the company of Reis, we discover the city's landmarks, a city of slopes and
lookouts dominating the waters of the Tagus. Posters, advertisements and a
wealth of visual detail provide a vivid picture of the city's commerce, the
trading companies and products of the day, the time-honoured traditions and
local customs, the numerous churches, convents, theatres, cinemas and
music halls. A city of bustle and sharp contrasts, a nation much given to
parades and processions, feast-days and carnival.

But once installed in the Hotel Bragança, a glass house at once confining
and transparent, 'lugar neutro, sem compromisso, de trânsito e vida suspensa'
(22), Reis gradually becomes aware of a clandestine Lisbon, of the anxieties and
fears lurking in the background. The political events that were to change the
face of Europe, notably the civil war in Spain and the upsurge of Fascism in
Italy and Germany, also began to affect Portugal. A tiny country with reduced
resources, Portugal could hope for little in the power game being played by
stronger nations. The repressive régime introduced by Salazar's 'New State'
aped the Fascist régimes of Italy and Germany with disastrous results. Salazar,
Portugal's self-styled sage, protector and gentle potentate, courted the
approval of these dubious allies, while leading his country into crippling
isolation. The spirit of patriotism he invoked was to absolve all excesses and
justify the most glaring contradictions.

Reis' pessimistic view of the political arena of the day and his contempt
for political expediency provide Saramago with an irresistible opportunity to
voice his own firm belief that deception is the very essence of politics:

Lutam as nações umas com as otras, por interesses que não são de
Jack nem de Pierre nem de Hans nem de Manolo nem de
Giuseppe, tudo nomes de homem para simplificar, mas que os
mesmos e outros homens tomam ingenuamente como seus, os
interesses, ou virão a sê-lo à custa de pesado pagamento quando
chegar a hora de liquidar a conta. (149)

The voice we are listening to here is that of a committed communist who knows that powerful neighbours can either offer help or extermination. As a political force, Portugal comes across as a nation that has lost its nerve and initiative; servile and ineffectual, timid even on her home territory, she is patronized by the rest of Europe and is insultingly typecast as the 'loyal ally'.

Saramago frequently refers to the tiny voice of Portugal, and this sense of inferiority conditions the Portuguese people both at home and abroad. The author reminds us that no one can claim to be truly Portuguese unless he speaks another language better than his own, a nation of emigrants prepared to settle wherever they can find something to eat and earn some money. Patient, hard-working and submissive, the Portuguese have mastered the art of self-effacement: 'este povo ainda tem na memória inconsciente os costumes do deserto, continua a acreditar que o que defende do frio defende do calor, por isto se cobre todo, como se se escondesse' (310). Brainwashed by the politicians and clergy, the people are encouraged to confuse things human and divine and to believe that 'Portugal é Cristo e Cristo é Portugal' (281).

Seen through the eyes of an atheist who is not insensitive to the persuasive influence of religion, the Holy Shrine of Fatima is yet further proof of human gullibility. The faith and resignation of the pilgrims returning empty-handed fills Reis with quiet rage and frustration. In search of a miracle, these pilgrims advance from every cardinal and collateral point until they converge at the shrine: 'Fátima ... uma enorme estrela ... esta preciosa jóia de catolicidade resplandece por muitos lumes ... sofrimento ... fé ... caridade ... a indústria de bentinhos e similares ... quinquilharia ... comes e bebes ... perdidos e achados' (317). A dispirited Reis retreats from the pilgrimage convinced that once we start believing in miracles we have lost all hope. Stoic resignation is preferable by far and will bring fewer disappointments: 'Não tentarás o Senhor teu Deus em a Senhora Sua Mãe e, se bem pensasses, não deverias pedir, mas aceitar, isto mandaria a humildade, só Deus é que sabe o que nos convém' (318).

Reis is equally scornful of that other major instrument of manipulation, the Press, which misleads its readers while satisfying their curiosity. Perusing the newspapers of the day, Reis uncovers yet another labyrinth of information at once significant and trivial, true and false, selected and edited for maximum effect and couched in words which conceal as much as they reveal, the language pitched at the level of the masses they hope to brainwash. Salazar transformed the Press into a powerful instrument of propaganda and self-aggrandizement. We are reminded that the ideals and achievements of the New State were constantly being extolled in the newspapers. Thanks to Salazar, Divine Providence was pouring endless blessings on Portugal while the rest of the world faced doom and destruction, a farcical travesty not unlike the special edition printed daily for the senile John D. Rockefeller which reported nothing but prosperity, the end of unemployment, the death of communism in Russia, and the virtues of the American way of life, while suppressing every item of bad news.

Returning from the relaxed, not to say lax, atmosphere of Brazil, it is perhaps inevitable that Reis should be struck by the persistent rigidity of the social hierarchy in his native Portugal. He has his own ironic theory about social harmony:

> a paz social é uma questão de tacto, de finura, de psicologia, para tudo dizer numa palavra só, à vez três vezes, se ela ou elas coíncídem rigorosamente com o pensamento é problema a cujo deslindamento já tínhamos renunciado. (217)

Beholding the spectacle of the world from his own privileged position, he is painfully aware of its ironies, injustices and inequalities. The lower orders, that backward clan, disconcert and exasperate him with their endless capacity for suffering and humiliation (whether it be sincere or false). Reis comments that if Lydia were not a maid at the Hotel Bragança, there is every possibility that she would make an excellent tightrope walker, juggler or musician, for she has talent enough for any of these professions. And this reflection squares with Saramago's firm conviction that even the most deprived members of society are exceptional human beings who only need the right conditions in order to show their true worth. Class distinctions are further explored when we meet the two women in Reis' life: the warm-hearted, uncomplaining Lydia who submits to the advances of hotel guests because 'a vida é triste', and the coy, elusive Marcenda who has the right social credentials but whose chances of a normal existence have been dashed by the embarrassing disfigurement of a withered arm. The presence of Lydia and Marcenda satisfies two quite separate strands in Reis' nature: a man in search of his creature comforts and sexual gratification on the one hand, the poet in search of the ideal muse on the other, because even poets, after all, are not exempt from the demands both of the flesh and the spirit. Reis' warring emotions on both counts tell us everything we need to know about accepted attitudes between men and women in a society fettered by religious beliefs and social prejudices. And our protagonist speaks with two voices: pursuing his muse one minute as he works at a poem and engaging in a little erotic combat the next to steady his nerves and calm his thoughts. Uneasy relationships between men and women are probed in all Saramago's books and with disarming honesty. He confides that there are moments in life when we think we are experiencing passion and it is merely an outburst of gratitude. His limited experience of women has taught him the difference between love and companionship, the latter seemingly preferable because less painful and demanding.

So much for the personal dimension as Reis renews contact with his past and intellectual formation, but what of the universal dimension surrounding the charismatic figure of Fernando Pessoa—poet, philosopher and a pervasive presence even as a ghost?

Saramago's portrait of Pessoa is accurate in every detail: a fastidious and somewhat enigmatic human being, a keen observer of life and hypersensitive by nature. As an intellectual, Pessoa was impressive. A man with wide interests, a voracious reader and attuned to new philosophical ideas and literary trends then current in Europe. Avant-garde journals published in Lisbon provided Pessoa with a platform for his theories about art and life. In his poetry and essays, there is a lingering sense of disquiet: 'Não conheço quem fui no que hoje sou'.[2] In dialogue, Reis, his heteronym, alternately identifies with Pessoa or questions his creator's conclusions on every imaginable issue from political allegiances to the essence of true love. And to complicate matters, the voice of Saramago himself can be heard intermittently, adding his own note of agreement or dissent. The dialogues between Pessoa and Reis are wary and tense, they confess to never having really understood each other as they recapitulate and reiterate their convictions, qualify and revise certain opinions they once held. In both men there is a contagious pessimism and weariness, Pessoa the more resigned, Reis the more irritable and sceptical, 'a mais duvidosa das pessoas' (361); both are keenly aware of their inner solitude, of a profound silence (the half-brother of solitude). Like Pessoa before him, Reis feels overwhelmed by the enormity of the world, by too much talk, too much literature, and he declares himself exhausted after hours of listening to

> os pulmões portugueses tuberculosos, cansado também de ter palmilhado a cidade, no espaço limitado por onde incessantemente circula, como a mula que vai puxando a nora, de olhos vendados, e, apesar disso ou por causa disso, sentindo por momentos a vertigem do tempo, o oscilar ameaçador das arquitecturas, a viscosa pasta do chão, as pedras moles. (267)

Here we find the same dark musings as in Pessoa's *Livro do Desassossego*, but offset by the simple need to believe that there are some good things in life such as love, for example, or that happiness which unhappy people are continually talking about. Yet for the self-questioning Pessoa and Reis, happiness and love might well prove to be impossible, given their difficulty in knowing themselves. And this is where Lydia shows her inner strength. She possesses neither Reis' intellect nor powers of introspection, but when it comes to knowing herself she does not appear to have the slightest doubt. Their relationship reveals the abyss between what Pessoa defines as 'vida teórica' and 'vida prática'.[3] The words she utters are simple and to the point, yet somehow more meaningful than the fastidious discussions of Pessoa and Reis: 'singular rapariga esta Lídia, diz as coisas mais simples e parece que as diz como se apenas mostrasse a pele doutras palavras profundas que não pode ou não quer pronunciar' (305).

The existential problem posed by Pessoa, Reis and Saramago, is that every human being is individual while resembling every other human being. We are all unique, yet innumerable, and this multiple personality exacerbates the problem of self-identity and our fragmentation. To complicate matters, the gods, too, are innumerable, but hopefully superfluous: 'quem não tem Deus procura deuses, quem deuses abandonou a Deus inventa, um dia nos livraremos deste e daqueles' (73). This fragmentation means that we can feel many, often contradictory, things at the same time. And this in turn can so easily lead us into misunderstanding and misinterpretation; human error and its dire consequences being one of Saramago's constant preoccupations.

Another obsessive preoccupation is the thought of encroaching death. Man is compared with an elephant that senses its approaching end. A constant theme in his poetry and prose while alive, death is perceived somewhat differently by the Pessoa who returns from the grave. The poet's confidences to Reis give as much cause for disquiet as reassurance. Looking back on life, Pessoa can best describe it as a lingering convalescence:

> afinal a vida não é muito mais que estar deitado, convalescendo
> duma enfermidade antiga, incurável e recidívante, com intervalos
> a que chamamos saúde, algum home lhes havíamos de dar, vista a
> diferença que há entre os dois estados. (171)

This uneasy pact between life and death extends to that between memory and oblivion, and Pessoa warns Reis that the wall separating the living from one another is no less opaque than the wall that separates the living from the dead. The poet's message would appear to be that, when the laughter and the tears have subsided, we are left with shadows, a sense of futility, a shaming recognition of our own ineptitude when it comes to accepting fundamental truths, and when Reis accuses Pessoa of trivial philosophizing, he warns him that everything loses its significance once seen from his side of death.

Convinced that the works of mankind are ever incomplete, Pessoa can attest to lost opportunities, to missing out on that one word that needed to be said, that one gesture that needed to be made before time ran out. Once dead, Pessoa becomes aware that being and existing are not the same thing, and that in the final analysis none of us is truly alive or dead, nor is anyone the wiser as to whether 'this passing shadow we cast on the ground is life because it resembles life'.

Pessoa's lifelong concern with the inevitability of fate is echoed throughout Saramago's novel. We are constantly being reminded that no man escapes his ironic destiny—'o destino, além de obreiro, também sabe de ironias' (258)—or can hope to win his battle against time: 'Não há resposta para o tempo, estamos nele e assistimos nada mais' (323). As Ricardo Reis lies in bed, he imagines that he can see the palm of God's hand overhead and is reading there the lines of life, of a life that narrows, is interrupted and revived, becomes more and more tenuous, a besieged heart solitary behind those walls. In Saramago's firmament the gods are wise and indifferent, and above them is fate, the supreme order to which even gods are subject. Once he touches on the divinities, Saramago becomes cynical, rebellious, and subversive. Because the gods of Ricardo Reis are silent, unfeeling entities prepared to dupe and abandon us:

> para quem o mal e o bem são menos que palavras, por as não dizerem eles nunca, e como as diriam, se mesmo entre o bem e o mal não sabem distinguir, indo como nós vamos no rio das coisas, só deles distintos porque lhe chamamos deuses e às vezes acreditamos. (60)

The challenge confronting mankind is to change fate without the assistance of god or gods, to change it for better or worse, and to prevent fate from being fate.

In Saramago, critics worldwide have recognized a master of irony, a writer with an unsparing eye for human foibles and paradoxical situations. And when pressed on this point he once explained: 'I de-dramatise life through irony'.[4] In *O Ano da Morte de Ricardo Reis*, the registers of parody and satire are as unpredictable as they are varied. Saramago can be biting yet compassionate, discerning yet deeply moving. His most bitter remarks are directed at the powerful and affluent who live in dread of some dangerous subversion of social class and ranking, a thing greatly to be feared. New Year resolutions, he insists, are only for the common people: the others, uncommon and superior, have their own good reasons for being and doing quite the opposite whenever it suits or profits them. Mindful of the time-honoured rivalry between Spain and Portugal, Reis mentally compares the subdued mutterings and whispers of the Portuguese with the high-pitched voices of wealthy Spanish refugees speaking the sonorous language of Cervantes and flaunting their triumph in misfortune: his disgruntled thoughts echoing time-honoured grievances: 'os espanhóis são assim, querem logo tomar conta de tudo, é preciso estar sempre de olho neles' (393). The English fare no better. Perfidious Albion, we are reminded, has lived up to her reputation and given nearly every other nation just cause for complaint, and when Reis sees cricket being played on the deck of the ocean liner *The Highland Brigade*, he is even more convinced that for the British Empire nothing is impossible. The author can be engagingly witty when he suggests that the only real justification for statues is to provide perches for pigeons or suggests that Bovril might be the answer to the country's poverty, as he watches leaflets advertising the beverage's nutritious value dropping from the clouds on to the pilgrims at Fatima. The humour becomes rumbustious, not to say risqué, when Reis finally kisses the highly-strung Marcenda and can feel the blood rushing to his temples and his libido aroused, and there is a hint of playful irreverence when he retells the story of Adam and Eve and settles for an earthier vision of Paradise and its delights:

> Onde se reunirem homem e mulher, Deus estará entre eles, por estas novas palavras aprenderemos que o paraíso, afinal, não era onde nos tinham dito, é aqui, ali aonde Deus terá de ir, de cada vez, se quiser reconhecer-lhe o gosto. (224)

At times the humorist is reined in by the radical sceptic: 'Um homem, se estudou, aprende a duvidar, muito mais sendo os deuses tão inconstantes, certos apenas, eles por ciência, nós por experiência, de que tudo acaba, e o sempre antes do resto' (218). Life is looked at obliquely and with a questioning eye. But note that even the aloof and indifferent Reis is often stirred by unexpected emotions to the extent of finding himself quaking because a simple cloud has passed.

Like all important novels, *O Ano da Morte de Ricardo Reis* is also a book about reading and writing. Note the titles of the two books mentioned several times within the narrative: *The God of the Labyrinth* and *Conspiracy*, both titles embodying key themes throughout the novel. Drawing a clear distinction between the essential books and those which satisfy our inclinations, the author likes to think of his own books as a conversation with his reader. He frequently addresses the reader directly in mid-narrative, taking care to adopt a tone of voice which is challenging rather than confessional. This desire to be an 'oral narrator' has influenced his technique with its disregard for conventional punctuation. As he himself has stressed: 'the words written by me are intended as much to be read as to be heard ... the oral narrator speaks as if he were composing music and uses the same elements as the musician: sounds and pauses, high or low, some short, others long'.[5] As readers, we are invited to ponder and tease out the contradictions he exposes, to probe the nuances of the words and moments of silence. To complicate matters, *thinking itself* intervenes as if it were a protagonist, and like the Argentinian writer, Jorge Luis Borges, the author believes there is no more elaborate pleasure than that of thought. He makes frequent use of Borgesian images: the labyrinth, the chessboard, the compass, the river of time and the mirror, but the wealth of associations attributed to the last of these images shows just how skilfully he adapts these borrowings:

> talvez no espelho se tenha falado uma língua diferente, talvez outras palavras se tenham dito naquele cristalino lugar, então outros foram os sentidos expressos, parecendo que, como sombra, os gestos se repetiam, outro foi o discurso, perdido na inacessível dimensão, perdido também, afinal o que deste lado se disse, apenas conservados na lembrança alguns fragmentos, não iguais, não complementares, não capazes de reconstituir o discurso inteiro, o deste lado, insista-se, por isso os sentimentos de ontem não se repetem nos sentimentos de hoje, ficaram pelo caminho, irrecuperáveis, pedaços de espelho partido, a memória. (175–76)

Like Borges he specializes in tactical subtleties, dialectical cunning and rhetorical digressions. Saramago exploits philosophical preambles and frequent digressions to show just how deeply the human mind can burrow: 'a sensibilidade das pessoas tem recônditos tão profundos que, se por eles nos aventurarmos com ânimo de tudo examinar, há grande perigo de não sairmos de lá tão cedo' (122). As a writer he is motivated by the desire to establish patterns of symmetry amidst the chaos, to discover unexpected links between men and symbols; sometimes all too transparent, for example, a new automobile named The Dictator, or Marcenda's withered arm seen as a symbol of collective mutilation; at other times startlingly unreal, for instance, the image of St Francis of Assisi's stigmata linking him with the cross of Christ, and the crosses on the armbands of bank employees at a political rally.

In linguistic matters, Saramago is scrupulous, analysing, dissecting and contrasting words and their meaning; establishing different layers of meaning; investigating new formulations. He is particularly sensitive to words spoken from the heart as opposed to platitudes devoid of any human interest, and he leads us through an intricate mental process that derives from a succession of stimuli, sometimes unconscious, sometimes only pretending to be unconscious, which achieves new relationships of thought and expression. As with most of the important writers of our age, he cultivates that opacity of language whereby books are made out of words as much as out of characters and incidents. He neatly defines the tyranny of words:

> por que será que as palavras se servem tantas vezes de nós, vemo-las a aproximarem-se, a ameaçarem, e não somos capazes de afastá-las, de calá-las, e assim acabamos por dizer o que não queríamos, é como o abismo irresistível, vamos cair e avançamos. (214)

Yet much as he is worried by the inauthenticity of language and the danger of counterfeit emotions, he reassures us in the next breath that words are the best tools we can hope for in our attempt, ever frustrated, to express what we call thought. Language, for Saramago, owes much of its fascination to the inherent contradictions, and he warns us that unless we are prepared to use all words, however absurd, we will never say the essential words. The texture of his own prose owes much of its richness to multiple registers as he goes from description to philosophical speculation, from melancholy and despair to wry humour. By restricting punctuation to commas and full-stops, he creates his own verbal music and allows for a greater variety of inflections. The basic technique is that of counterpoint as he sets up a game of voices, each voice establishing its own truths, yet truths often saying different things.

Connecting the threads across time (a time at once linear and labyrinthine), finding certain threads without knots and certain knots without threads, Saramago shows us how the past and its ghosts can be more real and concrete than life in the present.

For Saramago, writing novels is a truly passionate way of living life and enlarging on the world. He does not subscribe to the idea of an absent, impartial narrator. In *O Ano da Morte de Ricardo Reis* our author is omniscient and omnipresent, and he shows an almost carnal relationship with his country and people while transcending all barriers of race and culture in his pursuit of a vision of totality. The novelist's art, as he understands and practises it, is not one of reflection or imitation but a skilful act of invention:

> O objecto da arte não é a imitação ... a realidade não suporta o seu reflexo, rejeita-o, só uma outra realidade, qual seja, pode ser colocada no lugar daquela que se quis expressar, e, sendo diferentes entre si, mutuamente se mostram, explicam e enumeram a realidade como invenção que foi, a invenção como realidade que será. (109–10)

Or as Pessoa himself expressed it: 'Sobre a nudez forte da verdade o manto diáfano da fantasia' (62).

As in all of his major novels, the author's earthly journey leads him irresistibly back to the point of departure. The opening phrase—'Aqui o mar acaba e a terra principia' (11)—finds its completion in the closing sentence: 'Aqui, onde o mar se acabou e a terra espera' (415). Sea and earth, space and time, past and present merge in this kaleidoscopic vision of an awesome totality.

NOTES

1. José Saramago, *O Ano da Morte de Ricardo Reis* (Sixth Edition, Lisbon: Caminho, 1985), 118. All quotations are taken from this edition.

2. 'O Andaime', from the *Cancioneiro* in *Obra Poética* (Third Edition, Rio de Janeiro: José Aguilar Editora, 1969), 159.

3. Fernando Pessoa, *Livro do Desassossego*, edited by Vicente Guedes and Bernardo Soares (Lisbon: Editorial Presença Lda., 1990), 228.

4. Giovanni Pontiero: Interview with José Saramago, *PN Review*, XVI (1989), No. 4, 41.

5. *Ibid.*, 39.

DAVID FRIER

Ascent and Consent:
Hierarchy and Popular Emancipation in
the Novels of José Saramago

T he title of José Saramago's second novel, *Levantado do Chão*, published
in 1980, indicates a metaphorical rise from the ground, which represents
increasing control by ordinary people over their own lives. This idea is
central to the development of the novel as a whole. My intention is to explore
the relationship between such spatial imagery and political ideology in this
and other works by the novelist, and thus to suggest that the physical
movements of their protagonists should not be regarded merely as events in
the plot, but also as significant indicators of maturity and responsibility, at a
national as well as at a personal level.

It is my contention that the author's political beliefs, in some shape or
form, are a significant element in all of his works. The experiences recounted
in *Levantado do Chão* leave little doubt as to its essentially revolutionary
ideology: the Holy Trinity of Christian tradition finds itself parodied here in
the unholy alliance of Church, landowners and state, whose repressive
character has served to keep the people of Monte Lavre in submission for
generations.[1] To reinforce this point the author depicts a number of
subordinate power-structures which indicate a whole hierarchy, extending
down from the ruling classes and their institutionalized allies to a number of
disadvantaged groups. Thus, for example, as Marie-Eve Letizia has
illustrated at length, there is a particularly marked growth in the

From *Bulletin of Hispanic Studies*, vol. 71, no. 1 (January 1994). © 1994 Liverpool University
Press.

consciousness of women who move from an initial position of willing submission to prevailing social structures—and, in particular, to male dominance—to a situation where, by the end, the young Maria Adelaide is seen as the symbol of hope for further gains in the future.[2]

The power-structures which operate within the traditional community of Monte Lavre in the early part of *Levantado do Chão* are, therefore, not based on a simple opposition between oppressor and oppressed. Rather, as is indicated early in the novel by the potential conflict between the local labourers and the cheaper workforce brought in from the Beiras to take their place, there is a concerted attempt made by the authorities to enforce a system of 'divide-and-rule'. They seek thus to create a hierarchy of oppressors who are in turn oppressed by others, all of them ultimately under the control of the ruling classes, whose influence is evident in the arrival of the 'patrão' to give his silent approval to the work of the factor and the police sergeant (37–38). So Letizia's account of the gradual emancipation of women fits into a broader vision, a vision of the need for solidarity amongst all of the oppressed against the true oppressor. In this way a social order could be created which would be more just for all, reconciling differences between black and white (323) and between father and son (334–36), and also bringing an end to the specific problem discussed by Letizia, that of the exploitation of woman by man.

It is, therefore, the threat of conflict amongst brother-workers— suggested in the text itself by a casual reference to Cain and Abel (197)— which is seen to stand in the way of progress for the workers of Monte Lavre. As long as the divisions amongst the rural workers can be preserved, the privileged minority will remain invulnerable, as Father Agamedes insinuates, through archaic language and biblical echoes, in his words on seeing João Mau-Tempo in prison. These words suggest a divinely ordained and therefore immutable social hierarchy:

> Assim estaremos no céu, eu no centro como convém ao múnus espiritual que exerço desde que me conheço e me conheceis, vós tenente à minha direita por serdes protector das leis e de quem as faz, vós agente à sinistra minha por fazerdes o resto do trabalho, cujo não quero saber nem que me obriguem. (159)

And yet there are suggestions that this power-structure is not as impregnable as it might seem at first: most notably, Father Agamedes' very name is an allusion to the classical legend of Agamedes, who, along with his brother Trophonius, constructed the treasury of King Hyrieus of Boeotia in such a way as to ensure that they could obtain access and steal its treasures in secret, only to be trapped inside and beheaded. The implications for Monte Lavre are clear: Father Agamedes has been acting in complicity with his brothers in crime (the landowners) to defraud the legitimate owners of the land (the workers), who need only become aware of the crimes being perpetrated against them to be mobilized into protecting what is legitimately theirs: 'A grande e decisiva arma e a ignorância', as Sigisberto concedes (72).

Gradually the people do achieve emancipation, and it is significant that this development is linked repeatedly to physical movement upwards: in the earlier stages of the text, the landowners, who observe events from their castle atop the hill which gives Monte Lavre its name, seem impregnable, and this sense of security is linked not only to the idea of height, but also to that of breadth of vision, which at first is the exclusive property of the ruling classes:

> Quando Lamberto Horques Alemão subia ao eirado do seu castelo, não lhe chegavam os olhos para tanto ver ... Ele próprio, ali com sua mulher honrada e já seus filhos, haveria de espalhar semente aonde lhe aprouvesse. (26)

Only the landowners have a broader perspective, and only the landowners therefore can take a place on top of the hill in the sun, as João Mau-Tempo dreams of doing (96), and this advantage permits them to take all decisions as they see fit:

> De Monte Lavre, alto lugar, olham os donos do latifúndio as grandes vagas amarelas que rangem sob a mansa rajada do vento, e dizem para os feitores, É tempo de ceifar. (138)

Immediately, however, this decision is questioned by the refusal of the workers to labour for less than thirty-three escudos per day (138). The ordinary man and woman have thus begun their gradual ascent towards their ultimate position of control of their own destiny, so that by the latter part of the text, for example, when António speaks of going up to Montemor to demand a living wage, he does so after a symbolic climb to the heights which traditionally have been beyond the reach of his class (308); and from there, it is said (309), he may survey the whole earth, as his brothers and sisters grow in awareness of one another and of their common struggle.

The climb is not without its setbacks. Each step is a dangerous one, and, when the workers go too far, there is a price to be paid. When João

Mau-Tempo and his comrades Sigismundo Canastro and Germano Vidigal withhold their labour in the small community of Monte Lavre, the result is that they are taken up to Montemor (literally 'the larger mountain'), where Germano is said to be thrown back on the ground as he is tortured and ultimately killed (173–75). Significantly, the next time that João and Sigismundo meet, the narrator points out that they are on the Atalaia hill, but 'nao no alto'—some retrenchment and consolidation is needed before the next upward steps can be taken (207). These come when João is arrested and taken to Lisbon for interrogation on the third floor of a building which must seem like the Tower of Babel to a peasant accustomed to the single-storey architecture of the Alentejo (241); Father Agamedes' comment on João's arrest is to accuse him of sinful pride, which he describes as the worst of the mortal sins, 'porque é ele que levanta o homem contra o seu patrao e o seu Deus' (243). Clearly João is climbing to dangerous heights, and, as he is interrogated and maltreated, he can hardly continue to keep himself upright, whereas 'tudo quarto era igreja estava de pé e triunfante' (251).

The transition to more recent times and more dramatic changes is marked by the birth of Maria Adelaide to Gracinda Mau-Tempo and Manuel Espada. As a preliminary indication of the symbol of hope which her daughter is to become, Gracinda raises her from the ground as the menfolk discuss their plans to go to Montemor to demand their living wages (308). When they go there—in a procession which is presented ironically in terms of a Moorish siege of a Christian castle (310–11)—they are first thrown to the ground by the forces of the local authorities, but they then rise once more, like the irresistible force of the sea (313). On this occasion, although the powerful landowners search for the protesters, they cannot prevent António from remaining in Montemor, and, indeed, on the slopes of the castle-hill itself (317). Significantly, only four pages later we read that 'são os tempos novos que estão a vir muito depressa' (321).

Predictably, the old guard is less than delighted with these developments. Father Agamedes, faced with the loss of his traditional privileges, sees these events as a downward movement from his perspective (321), in terms of a rock rolling downhill out of control, while the ordinary people, long accustomed to accepting his word, react in the opposite way. Suddenly, 'há vozes que se põem de pé' (334), prepared to talk openly of rising from the ground (336), and the narrator writes of 'dois milhões de suspiros que se ergueram do chão' (364). The Revolution has come, and now, at last, it is the people themselves who can make their own new reality.

What is important, is that there has been a *collective* rise amongst the people of Monte Lavre and of Portugal as a whole, as indicated by the image of dogs barking in defiance of their masters—a metaphor which is sustained at regular intervals throughout the text and which could be related to the recovery of the long-lost bark of the dogs of Cerbère in the opening section of *A Jangada de Pedra*:

> Em todo o latifúndio só se ouve ladrarem cães. Ladraram quando entre o Minho e o Algarve, entre a costa do mar e a raia do levante se agitaram as populações ao nome e verbo do general, e ladraram um ladrar novo que em linguagem de gente significava, Se queres aumento de ordenado, vota no Delgado. (305)

The change in people's lives has been led by individuals such as João Mau-Tempo and Germano Vidigal, who have been prepared to move upwards into personal danger for their ideals. But the rise which ultimately is successful here is a gradual, collective effort. All of the workers involved in it must keep their feet on the soil of the community. This image, which recurs several times in the text, I would suggest, is intended to indicate the importance of remaining in contact with their legitimate base, that of the popular will. Thus, for example, Sigismundo Canastro in prison remains proudly and defiantly 'sentado no chão' (152). The decision taken by José Calmedo to abandon the police force out of shame after arresting João Mau-Tempo for being a communist comes after the former has seated himself on the ground and has laid down his arms (233). This desertion fulfils the earlier prophecy by the narrator:

> Um dia ... entregará ao comandante do poste de Monte Lavre ... o seu pedido de demissão, e irá com a mulher e os dois filhos para longe dali, aprenderá a assentar o pé no chão como um civil e levará o resto da vida a esquecer que foi guarda. (231)

Levantado do Chão, therefore, sums up the entire process of a growing political consciousness and emancipation in Monte Lavre and, by extension, in Portugal as a whole, over several generations. Amongst Saramago's novels this work is unique, being the only one which does not have a specific protagonist or protagonists, but instead—and, some might be tempted to say, in keeping with its ideological inspiration—a whole class of rural labourers as its focus. Moreover, the more recent novels concentrate on restricted moments in history. This concentration would seem to preclude the possibility of the type of broader analysis offered by the earlier work.

Should we, then, see the later works, with their focus upon the individual protagonist and the snapshot in time, as an indication of retreat from earlier ideological purity? Such a view would surely seem difficult to reconcile with Saramago's recent reaffirmation of his loyalty to the Portuguese Communist Party.[3]

I would prefer to explain this development differently, seeing it as a retreat from the *aesthetic* ideology of the neo-Realist movement which undoubtedly influenced the conception of *Levantado do Chão*. The seductive flights of fantasy which are evident in texts such as *Memorial do Convento* simply could not co-exist easily with the predominantly social documentary tone of *Levantado do Chão*. In fact, in view of the prominence which the element of fantasy and the narratorial voice develop in Saramago's more recent works, one might say that his conception of political commitment in writing has moved from a Realist to a Brechtian model, where it is precisely the implausibility of the plot of a work such as *A Jangada de Pedra* which allows it to function effectively at an allegorical level.

In terms of content, however, whereas *Levantado do Chão* presents a complete process of popular emancipation, the other works which I intend to discuss (principally *Memorial do Convento* and *A Jangada de Pedra*) are not a denial, but a development of the same ideas which informed the creation of the earlier work. In other words, although the later texts may be read separately, they should be considered as different panels on something like a medieval triptych, visions of humanity which complement one another— through the recurrence of symbolism and imagery—to form a whole which is greater than the sum of their parts.

At least with *Memorial do Convento*, which takes an unorthodox and rather irreverent view of the construction of the great convent at Mafra, it is not difficult to see traces of the author's ideological commitment. The very opening section unambiguously sets out to ridicule the pretensions of the court and to suggest a monarchy which is morally bankrupt, while, as the text develops, it becomes increasingly apparent that fiscal bankruptcy is avoided only through the exploitation of overseas colonies and the poor at home. Yet I believe that the political implications of this work extend beyond the mere reflection of social inequality which is immediately apparent. For *Memorial do Convento*, like Saramago's other novels, is not only fiction; it is also an exploration of the ways in which popular advancement may—and may not— be achieved.

The author's intentions are surely revealed in the way that he concentrates on the history of the humble couple Baltasar and Blimunda, treating the nobler classes as an object of ridicule and leaving the construction of the convent as merely a part of the background to the novel. In spite of its ideological implications, this preference cannot in itself indicate any specific means for bringing change to the lives of ordinary people. I would suggest, rather, that these matters are explored by Saramago through the sub-plot concerning the couple's involvement in Father Bartolomeu Lourenço de Gusmão's obsessive plans to construct a flying-machine. This machine—whose ability to rise off the ground allows it to reach altitudes which dwarf even the megalomaniacal towers of the convent—seems at first to contrast with the royal project in that it is fuelled by the wills of ordinary people, for Blimunda possesses extraordinary powers of eyesight which permit her to 'see' human wills as dark clouds inside the bodies of other people and to 'collect' them in globes provided for this purpose, as Bartolomeu explains to her:

> o éter não se compõe das almas dos mortos, compõe-se, sim, ouçam bem, das vontades dos vivos ... Tirou do alforge um frasco de vidro que tinha presa ao fundo ... uma pastilha de âmbar amarelo. Este âmbar, também chamado electro, atrai o éter, andarás sempre com ele por onde andarem pessoas ... e quando vires que a nuvem vai sair de dentro delas ... aproximas o frasco aberto, e a vontade entrará nele. (123–24)[4]

The 'passarola' (as the machine is known) takes this otherwise ordinary couple on a flight in which they rise to dizzying heights at a speed which was impossible for the peasants in *Levantado do Chão*, and, like Christ tempted by the Devil, they see the world tantalizingly spread before them before they have to come back down to earth (196–203).

After the priest's disappearance, Blimunda will never again journey in the 'passarola', which seems likely to be left to decay. But Baltasar does make one further journey in it. When he goes to check on the condition of the machine several years later, he slips and it breaks free from its moorings to carry him up into the sky. After that we know nothing more of him until the very end of the text, when his lover finds him being burnt at the stake. Even then we are not told the reason for his execution, although it is presumably for witchcraft (356–57). It might seem surprising that, during the period of the couple's separation, Saramago chooses to follow the life of Blimunda on earth rather than what might be thought to be the more obviously attractive story of Baltasar in the skies. The fact that Saramago makes this choice indicates his preference for Blimunda's course of action. The real reason why Baltasar dies is that his flight is a symbolic one, indicating a loss of contact with everyday reality. He takes his example from Father Bartolomeu, who displays considerable 'hybris' as he exclaims during the maiden flight of the machine:

> ... se me visse el-rei, se me visse aquele Tomás Pinto Brandão que se riu de mim em verso, se o Santo Ofício me visse, saberiam todos que sou filho predilecto de Deus, eu sim, eu que estou subindo ao céu por obra do meu génio, por obra também dos olhos de Blimunda ... por obra da mão direita de Baltasar, aqui te levo, Deus, um que também não tem a mão esquerda. (196)

Significantly he then goes on to describe himself as God, Baltasar as the Son and Blimunda as the Holy Spirit (197), a claim whose presumption is instantly evident, given the difficulty which the three have in controlling the machine. Bartolomeu has already compared Baltasar to God on their first meeting, because, he claims, God too has no left hand—the hand which often, of course, is associated with evil (68)—a claim of which we are reminded by the narrator on various occasions (87, 169 and 185).

At a literal level, Baltasar is led to his doom by his carelessness in going back up in the flying-machine on his own, without the aid of Blimunda, who can perceive the wills which power it. Moreover, through repeated references to the classical legend of Icarus, who flew too close to the sun and fell back to earth to his death as a result, Saramago insinuates that Baltasar's fate is in some way a punishment. Even before the flying-machine is constructed, this legend is mentioned as Blimunda sees the irresistibility of rising to the maximum, height possible:

> Se o sol atrai o âmbar, e o âmbar atrai o éter, e o éter atrai o íman,
> e o íman atrai o ferro, a máquina irá sendo puxada para o sol, sem parar. (92)

Later she repeats the same warning in mid-air, while the inventor is still preoccupied entirely by his own achievement: 'Se não abrirmos a vela, continuaremos a subir, aonde iremos parar, talvez ao sol' (197). A further allusion to Icarus lies in Baltasar's own nickname 'Sete-sóis', which prompts him to remark:

> eu não sei desde quando e porquê nos meteram os sete sóis em casa, se fôssemos sete vezes mais antigos que o único sol que nos alumia, então devíamos ser nós os reis do mundo, enfim, isto são

conversas loucas de quem já esteve perto do sol e agora bebeu de
mais. (236)

The intoxication here mentioned is not only the result of alcohol.

Yet, one feels bound to ask just why Baltasar is subjected to this
punishment. The answer lies in a contrast, indicated earlier, which now turns
out to have been apparent rather than real. For both the construction of the
convent and the operation of Bartolomeu's flying machine involve upward
movement, and both involve the enslavement of others. In the king's project,
workmen are literally brought from all over the country to realize the
monarch's insane plans. Baltasar and Blimunda allow themselves—at first
quite innocently—to be hoodwinked into capturing people's wills and
imprisoning them in Bartolomeu's globes. Bearing these facts in mind, then,
Baltasar is seen to be as guilty of 'hybris' as Bartolomeu himself. In spite of
the latter's apparent sympathy for the couple who help him—telling a white
lie about their marital status, for example (119)—he functions as a
Mephistophelian figure in that he attempts to lure them into giving their
support to his insane plans, which ultimately lead Baltasar (as Faust) to his
downfall. Significantly, when Bartolomeu abandons him after their first
flight, Baltasar suspects that the priest may have been whisked away by
diabolical powers (206), but he none the less continues his involvement in
what is now clearly a doomed project.

Baltasar has been guilty of 'hybris' in two ways. Firstly, of course, he
and Blimunda have chosen to live outside the accepted structures of their
society by choosing not to marry, long before such practices became
acceptable. Perhaps what is more significant, however, is that, after
Bartolomeu's disappearance, they presume to maintain control of his flying
machine, which is powered by the wills of two thousand people: Blimunda
questions the legitimacy of this, but Baltasar dismisses her concern,
ultimately for reasons of personal vanity:

> Baltasar perguntou, Foste ver as vontades, Fui, respondeu ela, E
> estão lá, Estão, Às vezes penso que devíamos abrir as esferas, e
> deixá-las ir, Se as deixarmos ir, será como se não tivéssemos
> nascido, nem tu, nem eu, nem o padre Bartolomeu Lourenço,
> Continuam a parecer-se com nuvens fechadas, São nuvens
> fechadas. (271)

Baltasar has been seduced by the temptations of glory just as the king is—and
he no longer regards the wills as wills, but merely as what their physical

appearance indicates that they are, dark clouds; Baltasar is guilty of taking the owners of these wills for granted as much as the king is in requisitioning labour for the construction of the convent. Moreover, even granting his goodwill, he is simply not capable of controlling the flying machine. His stump of an arm does not, in fact, indicate divine status as Father Bartolomeu wrongly suggests. Rather it indicates his inadequacy for flying. In reaching this interpretation one is influenced by the description of the withered arm of the submissive Marcenda as 'uma ave doente, asa quebrada, chumbo cravado no peito' in *O Ano da Morte de Ricardo Reis*.[5] In common with his Old Testament namesake, then, the writing is on the wall for Baltasar because of his presumption, as the narrator himself insinuates:

> ... esse Baltasar não é o Mateus que conhecemos, mas sim aquele outro que foi rei de Babilónia, e que, tendo profanado, num festim, os vasos sagrados do templo de Jerusalém, por isso veio a ser punido, morto ás mãos de Ciro, que para a execução dessa divina sentença tinha nascido. (288)[6]

Baltasar's final journey in the 'passarola' is matched by another, the journey made by João Elvas to accompany that of the court to the Spanish border to celebrate two arranged Royal marriages. Interestingly, just as the efforts to raise the 'passarola' match the king's extravagant project at Mafra, so here the commoner's journey is said to be matched by the erection of an elaborate building specially for the occasion (304–05). The word 'erection' is perhaps particularly appropriate here, since shortly afterwards the forthcoming marriage is explicitly presented to one of the enforced brides in terms of brutal male domination (307).

The difference is that, whereas Baltasar's journey is vertical and solitary, João Elvas moves across the surface of the country, speaking to his compatriots, listening to them and learning from them wherever he goes. Baltasar, on the other hand, has been tempted by the spectacle shown to him by the priest. He presumes to keep the human wills imprisoned, thinking that he is capable of taking care of the ship on his own. To give further support to my negative interpretation of the meaning of the 'passarola', I would point to its successor, the Nazi airship which looms menacingly over Lisbon in *O Ano da Morte de Ricardo Reis*, representing a political doctrine which presumed to know the will of the people better than did the people themselves. In *Memorial do Convento* João also contrasts with Baltasar in that he is seen to be contributing to what will one day be a successful change— for the area which he passes through is precisely the area where *Levantado do*

Chão is set, and one of the people to whom he speaks is a certain Julião Mau-Tempo, who is even said to have blue eyes, one of the distinguishing marks of the Mau-Tempo family in the earlier novel (236).

Blimunda, in her turn, also undertakes a journey throughout Portugal in the latter stages of the book in search of her lost man. In the course of this journey she experiences many adventures, meets many people, defends herself valiantly against an attempted rape by a friar (345–46), and talks to the people wherever she goes, raising new questions and questioning established hierarchies:

> Por onde passava, ficava um fermento de desassossego, os homens não reconheciam as suas mulheres, que subitamente se punham a olhar para eles, com pena de que não tivessem desaparecido, para enfim poderem procurá-los ... Nunca entrava em igreja se havia gente lá dentro, apenas para descansar sentada no chão ou apoiada a uma coluna, entrei por um momento, vou-me embora já, esta não é a minha casa. Os padres que ouviam falar dela mandavam-lhe recados para que viesse à confissão, curiosos de saber que mistérios se ocultavam naquela romeira e peregrina ... A esses mandava dizer que fizera promessa de só confessar quando se sentisse pecadora, não poderia encontrar resposta que mais escandalizasse, se pecadores todos nós somos, porém, não era raro que falando sobre isto com outras mulheres as deixava pensativas, afinal, que faltas são essas nossas ... se nós somos, mulheres, verdadeiramente, o cordeiro que tirará o pecado do mundo. (354)

She has avoided taking the easy upward route. It is people like Blimunda, and João Elvas, who are slowly, painstakingly carrying out a gradual change in the circumstances of the society in which they live. Significantly, when she does finally find her Baltasar again, he has been raised on the stake in punishment for his past. But he has at least learnt from his mistake, for at the last moment, when Blimunda calls his will from his dying body, he chooses not to ascend into Heaven as the Church would wish, but to remain on the horizontal plane:

> E uma nuvem fechada está no centro do seu corpo. Então Blimunda disse, Vem. Desprendeu-se a vontade de Baltasar Sete-Sóis, mas não subiu para as estrelas, se à terra pertencia e a Blimunda. (357)

At the last, then, Baltasar is united with Blimunda. 'Sete-sóis' has been incorporated into 'Sete-luas', perhaps signifying a long-term approach, rather than a short-term one. Instead of tempting fate by soaring to the sun, Blimunda sees just enough in the moonlight to defend herself against the friar who attempts to rape her (345), an action which at a symbolic level indicates resistance to the institutional weight of the Church, as also represented by the huge stone intended for the convent which crushes the innocent Francisco Marques to death (259). Blimunda's way of less spectacular, but more meaningful, action offers raised awareness in the community at large and increased hope that one day a truly just, a truly classless society will be built.

A vision of the kind of solution which the novelist envisages in the longer term is perhaps evident in another of his works, *A Jangada de Pedra*, whose publication in 1986 coincided with the admission of Spain and Portugal into the EEC. Unlike the other novels examined here, this work has a contemporary setting, and there is no vertical axis immediately evident. The movement is wholly concentrated on the horizontal plane, as a small group of Portuguese and Spaniards take the opportunity of the changed circumstances of their Peninsula to engage in a journey of internal discovery. There are here, however, brief instances of what has been seen to be represented by the vertical axis in other works: the elimination by the authorities of the lone sailor who finds himself unexpectedly sailing into a deserted Lisbon (234),[7] and the interrogation of Joaquim Sassa and Pedro Orce (116). But one of the most striking features of this work is the extent to which the traditional hierarchy has been thrown into confusion by the unpredictable movements of the Iberian Peninsula: the poor and homeless take over holiday hotels in the Algarve in spite of the efforts of the police and the army to evacuate them (102–05); even the most powerful governments on earth are seen to be hopelessly incapable of reacting to the events which they cannot control (281–84); and the government of Portugal cannot even find any of its usual hollow words to react to the apparent crisis (223).

The crisis is, however, only an apparent one, for the dominant tone of the latter parts of the text is one of opportunity and hope for the future. The suggestion is made that it is the Iberian Peninsula, which is itself presented as being like a foetus approaching birth (319), which has impregnated all of the fertile women on its soil (319) in what is described as being an 'explosão genésica, uma vez que ninguém acredita que a fecundação colectiva tenha sido de ordem sobrenatural' (321). This statement would seem to be an allusion to the Virgin Birth, suggesting that the real route of Redemption lies in achieving one's own development rather than trusting in any hierarchical order. Further reinforcing this impression is the implicit equation of the Peninsula with an alternative Christ. On their peregrinations around the horizontal plane of Iberia, the five travellers decide to go up together and see the breach in the Pyrenees which has effectively placed them in control of their own destiny:

> Ao menos, estes viajantes sabem que se quiserem veros Pirinéus terão mesmo de lá chegar, pôr-lhes a mão emcima, que o pé não basta, por ser menos sensível, e os olhos, muito mais do que se julga, deixam-se enganar. (268)

These modern-day doubting Thomases have thus to put their hands into the wounded side of their homeland. The vision when they look down over the edge to behold their new-found status as an island will give them faith in following their own path, and not one set out for them by the more distant powers of Europe. At the very same moment, the Peninsula finally comes to a halt (296), with its new location between Africa and America reflecting its past history of exploration (322).

Once again, much of the enlightenment gained by the protagonists of *A Jangada de Pedra* is gained from discussions amongst the travellers, frequently while seated on the ground, in contact with the soil of Iberia: 'Estão sentados à sombra de uma árvore' (241), 'Estão sentados, felizmente numa sombra de árvores' (123). Earlier we see Joaquim, José and Pedro Orce seated in the shade of an olive tree, symbolizing peace and understanding (47), just as Jesus is seen twice in *O Evangelho Segundo Jesus Cristo*.[8] The significance which Saramago attributes to discussions of this kind may be deduced from other sources such as his *Viagem a Portugal*, where he writes: 'O viajante viajou no seu país. Isto significa que viajou por dentro de si mesmo, pela cultura que o formou e está formando'.[9] Travelling on the horizontal—not so much in a literal sense, but more in the metaphorical sense of promoting a fruitful exchange of ideas and offering mutual cultural refreshment—is what Saramago sees as being the future for the two Iberian nations. He indicates this same view more explicitly in an article in the journal *Vértice*, where he proposes new ideas of cultural contact to supersede nineteenth-century notions of 'Iberismo' and late twentieth-century plans for European union.[10] The countries which once led European overseas expansion and colonialism—a political system which existed on a clearly hierarchical basis—now have the opportunity to lead the way in showing popular emancipation as a viable alternative to the existing order. No wonder then that in *A Jangada de Pedra* the people of Europe show their solidarity with their erstwhile Iberian neighbours through the necessarily underground medium of graffiti which declare in a multitude of languages the message: 'We too are Iberians' (162–63).

The work closes with the death and burial of Pedro Orce, who has made love to both Maria Guavaira and Joana Carda, so that he too could be regarded as the father of the children which they now expect. In a sense, however, this amounts to the same thing as parentage by the Peninsula, for old Pedro Orce, the man who shares his name with the site of the oldest human remains to be found in the Peninsula, is surely intended to be a specifically Iberian representation of the old man as the Jungian archetypal representative of wisdom.

When Pedro Orce is buried, the, staff of Portuguese willow, which throughout has been associated with Joana Carda, is placed in Spanish soil to mark his grave, and the novel closes with a positive allusion to the biblical rod of Aaron which marked his tribe out as having a special duty towards God:[11] 'Os homens e as mulheres, estes, seguirão o seu caminho, que futuro, que tempo, que destino. A vara de negrilho está verde, talvez floresça no ano que vem' (330).

This is, of course, a statement of hope, but like Camões in *Os Lusíadas*—a work which in many ways is paralleled and parodied by the Iberian odyssey of *A Jangada de Pedra*—Saramago does not turn a statement of faith in his people into a simplistic declaration of easy achievement, for the word 'talvez' figures strongly. To conclude, I turn to a quotation from Saramago's television interview with Carlos Cruz in July 1993, where the novelist declared:

> O que nos faz falta talvez mais do que uma carta dos direitos humanos hoje é uma carta de deveres humanos, porque disso ninguém fala. O Comunismo para mim seria sempre (ou será quando for) um sistema social de responsabilidade colectiva, de interresponsabilidade em que cada pessoa é responsável por todas as pessoas.[12]

In the course of this interview José Saramago rejected categorically the hierarchical practices of Communism in the former Soviet Union and its satellites. What remains clear, however, is that he sees Communism as a means not of restricting, but of empowering the individual. I would suggest, therefore, that, while some of his novels concentrate on the negative course which, as he sees it, Portugal, and Western society in general, have followed until now, his work also outlines a more positive path forward. To take that path, the people themselves must not only be liberated but also be emancipated to assume responsibility, that is, they must be made ready to take on responsibility for the good of others. Baltasar's apparent liberation through the 'passarola' in *Memorial do Convento*, because it benefits only Baltasar himself, is seen to be as inadequate and fruitless as the king's construction of the convent. Along with liberation, therefore, the people must also accept responsibility.

In his vision Saramago sees the former colonial powers of Spain and Portugal, with their cultural links with Africa and Latin America, as having a special responsibility, in international terms, to bring about the development of this more emancipated community. The novelist's view is reflected in the external journey of the Peninsula itself in *A Jangada de Pedra*, while, internally, the greatest discovery made by the protagonists of this novel is the potential of their own voice—their ability to create change in their own lives. José Saramago sees his alternative vision of an emancipated Iberian society as being feasible—not in terms of specific political structures but rather in terms of a general culture of democracy—if the Portuguese and Spanish people are prepared to make it happen. The opportunity is there to be grasped, but Saramago emphasizes, in his reference to 'deveres humanos', that the people of Iberia themselves must constantly tend the plant which grows on Pedro Orce's grave.

NOTES

1. This is a metaphor which is used by Saramago himself within the text (see *Levantado do Chão* [Eighth Edition, Lisbon: Caminho, 19881, 223–24). All references to the text are taken from this edition. His ironic allusion to the Holy Trinity is also implicit in the speech of Sigisberto reported earlier in the text: 'este mundo é o único possível, tal como está, que só depois de morrer haverá paraíso, o padre Agamedes que explique isto melhor, e que só o trabalho dá dignidade e dinheiro ... foi Deus que quis assim as coisas, o padre Agamedes que explique melhor ... e se o padre não for suficiente, pede-se aí à guarda que dê um passeio pelas aldeias, só a mostrar-se, é um recado que eles entendem sem dificuldade' (72).

2. Marie-Eve Letizia, 'O lugar da mulher dentro do espaço e o processo da sua conscientização através da narrativa *Levantado do Chão* de José Saramago', in *Taira* (Grenoble: Centre de Recherche et d'Études Lusophones et Intertropicales, 1991), No. 3, 157–76.

3. Interview with Carlos Cruz, *Carlos Cruz na Quarta-Feira*, RTP, 28 July 1993.

4. References to *Memorial do Convento* are taken from the Nineteenth Edition (Lisbon: Caminho, 1989).

5. *O Ano da Morte de Ricardo Reis* (Sixth Edition, Lisbon: Caminho, 1985), 127.

6. The biblical tale of Belshazzar may be found in the Book of Daniel, chapter 5.

7. References to *A Jangada de Pedra* are from the First Edition (Lisbon: Caminho, 1986).

8. *O Evangelho Segundo Jesus Cristo* (Second Edition, Lisbon: Caminho, 1991), 185 and 251.

9, *Viagem a Portugal* (Second Edition, Lisbon: Caminho, 1990), 7.

10. See José Saramago, 'A Península Ibérica entre a Europa e a América Latina', in *Vértice*, 2nd series (March–April 1992), No. 47, 5–11.

11. The story of Aaron's rod may be found in the Book of Numbers, chapter 17, verses 1–10.

12. Interview with Carlos Cruz, *Carlos Cruz na Quarta-Feira*, RTP, 28 July 1993.

HAROLD BLOOM

"The One With the Beard Is God, the Other is the Devil"

I

José Saramago published *The Gospel According to Jesus Christ* in 1991, when he approached his seventieth year. As Saramago's fierce critical admirer, I am reluctant to choose it over all his other novels, but it is an awesome work, imaginatively superior to any other life of Jesus, including the four canonical Gospels. It loses some aspects of irony in Giovanni Pontiero's fine translation, but more than enough survives to overcome the aware reader.

Saramago's audacity is triumphant in his *Gospel* (the short title that I will employ). God, in Saramago's *Gospel*, has some affinities to the J Writer's Yahweh and some to Blake's Nobodaddy, but it is important to see that Saramago resists giving us the Gnostics' Ialdaboth. Kierkegaard in his *Concluding Unscientific Postscript* ironically observed that "to give thinking supremacy over everything else is gnosticism" (341). Yet Saramago's God scandalizes us in ways that transcend the intellect, since a God who is both truth and time is the worst possible bad news. Saramago's devil, delightfully named Pastor, is mildness itself compared to Saramago's God, who refuses Pastor's attempt to be reconciled, and who manifests neither love nor compassion for Jesus or for any other human being.

That must make the book seem sublimely outrageous, yet it is not, and

From *Portuguese Literary & Cultural Studies 6. On Saramago* (Spring 2001). © 2001 University of Massachusetts Dartmouth.

I think that only a bigot or a fool would judge Saramago's *Gospel* to be blasphemous. Saramago's God can be both wily and bland, and he has a capacity for savage humor. No one is going to love this god, but then he doesn't ask or expect love. Worship and obedience are his requirements, and sacred violence is his endless resource. Baruch Spinoza insisted that it was necessary for us to love God without ever expecting that God would love us in return. No one could love Saramago's God, unless the lover were so deep in sado-masochism as to be helpless before its drive.

God tells us in the Gospel that he is dissatisfied with the small constituency provided him by his chosen people, the Jews:

> For the last four thousand and four years I have been the God of the Jews, a quarrelsome and difficult race by nature, but on the whole I have got along fairly well with them, they now take Me seriously and are likely to go on doing so for the foreseeable future. So, You are satisfied, said Jesus. I am and I am not, or rather, I would be were it not for this restless heart of Mine, which is forever telling Me, Well now, a fine destiny you've arranged after four thousand years of trial and tribulation that no amount of sacrifice on altars will ever be able to repay, for You continue to be the god of a tiny population that occupies a minute part of this world You created with everything that's on it, so tell Me, My son, if I should be satisfied with this depressing situation. Never having created a world, I'm in no position to judge, replied Jesus. True, you cannot judge, but you could help. Help in what way. To spread My word, to help Me become the god of more people. I don't understand. If you play your part, that is to say, the part I have reserved for you in My plan, I have every confidence that within the next six centuries or so, despite all the struggles and obstacles ahead of us, I will pass from being God of the Jews to being God of those whom we will call Catholics, from the Greek. And what is this part You have reserved for me in Your plan. That of martyr, My son, that of victim, which is the best role of all for propagating any faith and stirring up fervor. God made the words martyr and victim seem like milk and honey on his tongue, but Jesus felt a sudden chill in his limbs, as if the mist had closed over him, while the devil regarded him with an enigmatic expression which combined scientific curiosity with grudging compassion. (311–12)

God is restless and does not wish to be depressed; those are his motives for victimizing Jesus, and subsequently for torturing to death the millions who will die as sacrifices to Jesus, whether they affirm him or deny him. That God is the greatest of comedians we learn from his chant of the martyrs: "a litany, in alphabetical order so as not to hurt any feelings about precedence and importance" (321). The litany is quite marvelous, from Adalbert of Prague, executed with a seven-pronged pikestaff, on to "Wolgefortis or Livrade or Eutropia the bearded virgin crucified" (325). Four long pages in length, the catalogue of sacred violence has such delights as Blandina of Lyons, gored by a savage bull, and the unfortunate Januaris of Naples, first thrown to wild beasts, then into a furnace, and finally decapitated. The gusto of Saramago's God recalls Edward Gibbon's in Chapter XVI of *The History of the Decline and Fall of the Roman Empire*, except that Gibbon, maintaining decorum, avoids detailing the many varieties of martyrdom by torture. But Gibbon again anticipates Saramago by observing that Christians "have inflicted far greater severities on each other than they had experienced from the zeal of infidels" (452–53). Saramago's God, his voice a little tired, speaks of the Inquisition as a necessary evil, and defends the burning of thousands because the cause of Jesus demands it. One blinks at the dustjacket of the American edition of Saramago's *Gospel*, where we are assured that defying the authority of God the Father "is still not denial of Him."

Though necessarily a secondary character in comparison to Saramago's Jesus, God demands scrutiny beyond his menacingly comic aspects. Primarily, the *Gospel's* God is time, and not truth, the other attribute he asserts. Saramago, a Marxist (an eccentric one), and not a Christian, subverts St. Augustine on the theodicy of time. If time is God, then God can be forgiven nothing, and who would desire to forgive him anyway? But then, the Gospel's God is not the least interested in forgiveness: he forgives no one, not even Jesus, and he declines to forgive Pastor, when the devil makes an honest offer of obedience. Power is God's only interest, and the sacrifice of Jesus employs the prospect of forgiveness of our sins only as an advertisement. God makes clear that all of us are guilty, and that he prefers to keep it that way. Jesus is no atonement: his crucifixion is merely a device by which God ceases to be Jewish, and becomes Catholic, a *converso* rather than a *marrano*. That is superb irony, and Saramago makes it high art, though to thus reduce it critically is to invite a Catholic onslaught. Of all fictive representations of God since the Yahwist's, I vote for Saramago's: he is at once the funniest and the most chilling, in the mode of the Shakespearean hero-villains: Richard III, Iago, Edmund in *King Lear*.

II

Pastor, or the devil, has his own charm, as befits a very original representation of Satan. A giant of a man, with a huge head, Pastor allows Jesus to become his assistant shepherd for a large flock of sheep and goats. In response to Jesus' Pious exclamation—"The Lord alone is God"—the non-Jewish Pastor replies with grand pungency:

> Certainly if God exists, He must be only one, but it would be better if He were two, then there would be a god for the wolf and one for the sheep, a god for the victim and one for the assassin, a god for the condemned man and one for the executioner. (192–93)

This sensible dualism is not exactly Satanic, and Pastor remains considerably more likeable than God throughout the novel. In the dialogues between the devil and the younger Jesus, the devil's part clearly prevails, though honorably, unlike God's dominance of Jesus when father and son first meet in the desert. God demands a sheep dear to Jesus as a sacrifice, and Jesus reluctantly assents. Pastor, on hearing of this, gives up on Jesus: "You've learned nothing, begone with you" (222). And Pastor, so far, is right: Jesus' education as to God's nature will be completed only upon the cross.

What then are we to make of Pastor? Saramago's devil is humane yet scarcely a skeptic: he knows too much about God. If Saramago's God is a Portuguese *converso*, then Saramago's devil was never Jewish, and seems curiously unrelated both to God and to Jesus Christ. Why is Pastor in the book? Evidently, only as a witness, I think one has to conclude. Saramago seems to take us back to the unfallen Satan of the Book of Job, who goes to-and-fro on the earth, and walks up and down on it. And yet Job's Satan was an Accuser; Pastor is not. Why does Jesus sojourn four years with Pastor, as an apprentice shepherd? The angel, who comes belatedly to tell Mary that Jesus is God's son tells us that "the devil only denies himself" (263), which is extravagantly ambiguous, and could mean that Pastor resists playing the role that God hag assigned him. Mary's angel, after telling us that Pastor was his schoolfellow, says that Pastor prospers because "the harmony of the universe requires it" (264). There is then a secret relationship between Pastor and God, a truth that dismays Jesus' disciples (302).

When God, dressed like a wealthy Jew, appears to Jesus in the boat, Saramago imagines a magnificent re-entry for Pastor:

The boat swayed, the swimmer's head emerged from the water, then his torso, splashing water everywhere, then his legs, a leviathan rising from the depths, and it turned out to be Pastor, reappearing after all these years. I've come to join you, he said, settling himself on the side of the boat, equidistant between Jesus and God, and yet oddly enough this time the boat did not tip to his side, as if Pastor had no weight or he was levitating and not really sitting, I've come to join you, he repeated, and hope I'm in time to take part in the conversation. We've been talking but still haven't got to the heart of the matter, replied God, and turning to Jesus, He told him, This is the devil whom we have just been discussing. Jesus looked from one to the other, and saw that without God's beard they could have passed for twins, although the devil was younger and less wrinkled. Jesus said, I know very well who he is, I lived with him for four years when he was known as pastor, and God replied, You had to live with someone, it couldn't be with Me, and you didn't wish to be with your family, so that left only the devil. Did he come looking for me or did You send him. Neither one nor the other, let's say we agreed that this was the best solution. So that's why, when he spoke through the possessed man from Gadara, he called me Your son. Precisely. Which means that both of you kept me in the dark. As happens to all humans. But You said I was not human. And that is true, but you have been what might technically be called incarnated. And now what do you two want of me. I'm the one who wants something, not he. But both of you are here, I noticed that Pastor's appearance came as no surprise, You must have been expecting him. Not exactly, although in principle one should always expect the devil. But if the matter You and I have to resolve affects only us, what is he doing here and why don't You send him away. One can dismiss the rabble in the devil's service if they become troublesome in word or deed, but not Satan himself. Then he's here because this conversation concerns him too. My son, never forget what I'm about to tell you, everything that concerns God also concerns the devil. (309–10)

As God and the devil are twins (we have suspected this), it is a delight to be told that we cannot live with God, and so must choose between our families and the devil. God speaks of his desire to be God of the Catholics, but this ambition I have glanced at already, and wish here only to ask: why is

Pastor in the boat? His expression combines "scientific curiosity with grudging compassion" (312), but he is there because, as Jesus accurately surmises, extending God's domain also extends the devil's. And yet poor Pastor has his perplexities:

> I'm staying, said Pastor, and these were the first words he spoke
> since revealing his identity. I'm staying, he said a second time,
> and added, I myself can see things in the future, but I'm not
> always certain if what I see there is true or false, in other words,
> I can see my lies for what they are, that is, my truths, but I don't
> know to what extent the truths of others are their lies. (318)

Saramago dryly calls this a "torturous statement," but he means that it clearly indicts God, whose truths indeed are his lies. God's account of the Catholic Church that will be founded upon Jesus is true only insofar as it is historically horrible, and the zest God manifests as he itemizes martyrs and sums up the Inquisition has unmistakable sadistic overtones. Most alarmingly, God (a good Augustinian, before Augustine) deprecates all human joys as being false, since all of them emanate from original sin: "lust and fear are weapons the demon uses to torment wretched mankind" (325). When Jesus asks Pastor whether this is true, the devil's reply is eloquently illuminating:

> More or less, I simply took what God didn't want, the flesh with
> all its joys and sorrows, youth and senility, bloom and decay, but
> it isn't true that fear is one of my weapons, I don't recall having
> invented sin and punishment or the terror they inspire.
> (325–26)

We tend to believe this when God snaps in response: "Be quiet ... sin and the devil are one and the same thing." Does it need God to say that? Wouldn't the Cardinal-Archbishop of Lisbon do as well? Saramago's reply is uncanny. God describes the Crusades, to be waged against the unnamed Allah, whom Pastor disowns creating:

> Who, then, will create this hostile god, asked Pastor. Jesus was at
> a loss for an answer, and God, who had been silent, remained
> silent, but a voice came down from the mist and said, Perhaps this
> god and the one to come are the same god. Jesus, God, and the
> devil pretended not to hear but could not help looking at one

another in alarm, mutual fear is like that, it readily unites enemies. (328–29)

Only here, in Saramago's *Gospel*, do we hear a voice beyond God's. Whose is it? Who could proclaim what God does not wish to say, which is that he and Allah are one? With a God as sly and unlovable as Saramago's, both we and Saramago long for a God beyond God, perhaps the Alien or Stranger God of the Gnostics. But whoever that God is, he does not speak again in this novel. Very deftly, Saramago has just told us explicitly what he tells us implicitly throughout: God and Jesus pragmatically are enemies, even as Pastor is the unwilling enemy of both. Yet in what does that enmity consist? Reacting to God's account of the Inquisition, Pastor remarks: "One has to be God to countenance so much blood" (330).

Pastor's great moment—and it is one of the handful of key passages in the book—comes in his vain attempt at reconciliation with God:

Pastor searched for the right words before explaining, I've been listening to all that has been said here in this boat, and although I myself have caught glimpses of the light and darkness ahead, I never realized the light came from the burning stakes and the darkness from great piles of bodies. Does this trouble you. It shouldn't trouble me, for I am the devil, and the devil profits from death even more than You do, it goes without saying that hell is more crowded than heaven. Then why do you complain. I'm not complaining, I'm making a proposal. Go ahead, but be quick, I cannot loiter here for all eternity. No one knows better than You that the devil too has a heart. Yes, but you make poor use of it. Today I use it by acknowledging Your power and wishing that it spread to the ends of the earth without the need of so much death, and since You insist that whatever thwarts and denies You comes from the evil I represent and govern in this world, I propose that You receive me into Your heavenly kingdom, my past offenses redeemed by those I will not commit in future, that You accept my obedience as in those happy days when I was one of Your chosen angels, Lucifer You called me, bearer of light, before my ambition to become Your equal consumed my soul and made me rebel against You. And would you care to tell Me why I should pardon you and receive you into My Kingdom. Because if You grant me that same pardon You will one day promise left and right, then evil will cease, Your son will not have to die, and Your kingdom will extend beyond the land of the Hebrews to embrace the whole globe, good will prevail everywhere, and I shall stand among the lowliest of the angels who have remained faithful, more faithful than all of them now that I have repented, and I shall sing Your praises, everything will end as if it had never been, everything will become what it should always have been. (330–31)

The irony of the humane Pastor and the inhumane God could not be better juxtaposed. God makes clear that he would prefer an even worse devil, if that were possible, and that without the devil, God cannot be God. Pastor, who has been persuasively sincere, shrugs and goes off, after collecting from Jesus the old black bowl from Nazareth into which the blood of Jesus will drip in the novel's closing words.

It is not sufficient to praise Saramago's originality in limning his wholly undiabolic devil. One must go further. The enigmatic Pastor is the only devil who could be aesthetically and intellectually appropriate as we conclude the Second Millennium. Except that he cannot be crucified, this fallen angel has far more in common with Saramago's Jesus than with Saramago's God. They both are God's victims, suffering the tyranny of time, which God calls truth. Pastor is resigned, and less rebellious than Jesus, yet that is because Pastor knows all there is to know. As readers, we remain more akin to Saramago's uncanny devil than we are to his malevolent ironist of a God.

III

The glory of Saramago's *Gospel* is Saramago's Jesus, who seems to me humanly and aesthetically more admirable than any other version of Jesus in the literature of the century now ending. Perhaps D.H. Lawrence's *The Man Who Died* is a near-rival, but Lawrence's Jesus is a grand Lawrencian vitalist, rather than a possible human being. Saramago's Jesus paradoxically is the novelist's warmest and most memorable character of any of his books. W.H. Auden, Christian poet-critic, oddly found in Shakespeare's Falstaff a type of Christ. I cite a paragraph of Auden to emphasize how far both Saramago's God and Saramago's Jesus are from even a generous, undogmatic Christian view:

The Christian God is not a self-sufficient being like Aristotle's First Cause, but a God who creates a world which he continues to love although it refuses to love him in return. He appears in this world, not as Apollo or Aphrodite might appear, disguised as man so that no mortal should recognize his divinity, but as a real man who openly claims to be God. And the consequence is inevitable. The highest religious and temporal authorities condemn Him as a blasphemer and a Lord of Misrule, as a bad Companion for mankind. Inevitable because, as Richelieu said, "The salvation of State is in this world," and history has not as yet provided us with any evidence that the Prince of this world has changed his character. (207–08)

Saramago's God, as I have said, neither loves the world nor does he expect it to love him in return. He wishes power, as widely extended as possible. And Saramago's Jesus is anything but an appearance of God "disguised as man"; rather his Jesus has been shanghaied by God, for God's own purposes of power. As for Satan, "the Prince of this world," we know that Saramago *has* changed his character.

The title of the novel is *The Gospel According to Jesus* Christ, where "according" matters most. Saramago's Jesus is an ironist, an amazingly mild one considering his victimization by God. Before meeting John the Baptist, Jesus is told that John is taller, heavier, more bearded, is hardly clothed, and subsists on locust and wild honey. "He sounds more like the Messiah than I do, Jesus said, rising from the circle" (354).

Saramago's novel begins and ends with the Crucifixion, *presented* at the start with considerable irony, but at the close with a terrible pathos:

Jesus is dying slowly, life ebbing from him, ebbing, when suddenly the heavens overhead open wide and God appears in the same attire He wore in the boat, and His words resound throughout the earth, This is My beloved son, in whom I am well pleased. Jesus realized then that he had been tricked, as the lamb led to sacrifice is tricked, and that his life had been planned for death from the very beginning. Remembering the river of blood and suffering that would flow from his side and flood the globe, he called out to the open sky, where God could be seen smiling, Men, forgive Him, for He knows nor what He has done. Then he began expiring in the midst of a dream. He found himself back in Nazareth and saw his father shrugging his shoulders and smiling as he told him, just as I cannot ask you all the questions, neither can you give me all the answers. There was still some life in him when he felt a sponge soaked in water and vinegar moisten his lips, and looking down, he saw a man walking away with a bucket, a staff over his shoulder. But what Jesus did not see, on the ground, was the black bowl into which his blood was dripping. (376–77)

"Men, forgive Him, for He knows not what He has done" testifies both to Jesus' *sweetness* and to Saramago's aesthetically controlled fury. No disinterested reader, free of ideology and of creed, is going to forgive Saramago's God for the murder of Jesus and the subsequent torrents of human blood that will result. Joyce's Stephen speaks of the "hangman God," as some Italians still call him, and that precisely is Saramago's God. This would be appalling enough in itself but is augmented by the long and loving portrait that Saramago gives of his Jesus.

The story of this Jesus begins and ends with an earthenware bowl, first presented to Mary the mother of Jesus by a beggar, an apparent angel. That bowl overflows with luminous earth, presumably unfallen; at the close it catches the blood of the dying Jesus. The beggar is God, rather than Pastor, and appears again to Mary in a dream-vision that is also a tryst. When Jesus is born, God manifests again as the third of three passing shepherds, bringing bread of an occult kind. One supposes that this is subtly akin to God's seed resulting in the flesh of Jesus, but so nuanced is Saramago that supposition sometimes needs to be evaded, in this mysterious book.

The thirteen-year-old Jesus leaves home because the Romans have crucified his father Joseph, an invention entirely Saramago's own, just as Joseph's partial complicity in Herod's massacre of the innocents is also Saramago's rather startling suggestion, and is another trouble for Jesus that sends him forth on his road. But why does Saramago so alter the story? Perhaps this most humane of all versions of Jesus has to suffer the darkness of two fathers, the loving, unlucky, and guilty Joseph, and the unloving, fortunate, and even guiltier God.

When the boy Jesus disputes with the doctors of the Law in the Temple, I am reminded again of how Augustinian Saramago has made both God and the Law. One doesn't quarrel with this anachronism, because Saramago's God is himself so anxious to forsake Judahism (to call it that) for Catholicism. And besides, one grants Saramago his anachronisms in this marvelous book just as one grants them endlessly to Shakespeare. Still, guilt is not a concern of the only traditional Jesus who moves me, the Gnostic Jesus of the Gospel of Thomas. Yet I am a Jewish Gnostic explicating a beautiful book by a Portuguese who is no Catholic, anymore than Fernando Pessoa was. At just this point in his narrative, Saramago brings Jesus and Pastor together, and that curious sojourn I have examined already.

And yet Jesus' principal relationship in his life, as Saramago sees it and tells it, is to neither of his fathers, nor to the devil, nor to Mary his mother, but to the whore Mary Magdalene. Of all the splendors of Saramago's Gospel, the love between Jesus and the Magdalene is the grandest, and their meeting and union (231–43) is for me the summit of Saramago's achievement, up to the present time. Echoing the Song of Songs, Saramago is most the artist when he intertwines a reply to Pastor with Jesus' awakening to sexual life:

> Jesus breathed so fast, for one moment he thought he would faint when her hands, the left hand on his forehead, the right hand on his ankles, began caressing him, slowly coming together, meeting in the middle, then starting all over again. You've learned nothing, begone with you, Pastor had told him, and who knows, perhaps he meant to say that Jesus had not learned to cherish life. Now Mary Magdalene instructed him.... (236)

We can void the "perhaps," and Mary Magdalene is Jesus' best teacher, eclipsing Joseph, God, Pastor, and Mary the mother. In what may be the book's greatest irony she teaches him freedom, which God will not permit any man, but in particular not to God's only son.

I myself have just turned seventy, and ask more urgently than before: where shall wisdom be found? The wisdom of Saramago's *Gospel* is very harsh: we can emulate Jesus only by forgiving God, but we do not believe, with Jesus, that God does not know what God has done.

I find the epilogue to Saramago's *Gospel* not in *Blindness*, a parable as dark as any could be, but in the charming *The Tale of the Unknown Island*, a brief fable composed in 1998, the year of his Nobel Prize, and translated a year later by Margaret Jull Costa. In the wonderful comic vein of *The Siege of Lisbon*, Saramago's tale begins with a man asking a king for a boat which can sail in quest of the unknown island. The boat granted, the man goes off to the harbor, followed by the king's cleaning woman, who will constitute the rest of the crew.

The cleaning woman, with superb resolution, vows that she and the man will be sufficient to sail the caravel to the unknown island, thus heartening the man, whose will cannot match hers. They go to bed in separate bunks, port and starboard, and he dreams bad dreams, until he finds her shadow beside his shadow:

> He woke up with his arms about the cleaning woman, and her arms about him, their bodies and their bunks fused into one, so

that no one can tell any more if this is port or starboard. Then, as soon as the sun had risen, the man and the woman went to paint in white letters on both sides of the prow the name that the caravel still lacked. Around midday, with the tide, The Unknown Island finally set to sea, in search of itself. (51)

Saramago names no one: I am critically outrageous enough to venture upon some experimental namings, as an antithesis to Saramago's *Gospel*. Let us call the man Jesus Christ, try the cleaning woman as Mary Magdalene, and the king, who exists to receive favors, will do for God. Doubtless, Saramago would shake his head, but so audacious a narrative genius inspires audacity in his critic. No one will be crucified upon the masts of the Unknown Island, and the bad dreams of *this* Jesus will not be realized. Saramago's happy tale is a momentary antidote to the most tragic of his works. Beware a God who is at once truth and time, Saramago warns us, and abandon such a God to sail out in search of yourself.

WORKS CITED

Auden, W.H. "The Prince's Dog." *The Dyer's Hand and Other Essays*. New York: Random House, 1962. 182–208.
Gibbon, Edward. *The History of the Decline and fall of the Roman Empire*. Vol. 1. New York Heritage Press, 1946.
Kierkegaard, Søren. *Concluding Unscientific Postscript to Philosophical Fragments*. Vol. l. Ed. and trans. Howard V. Hong and Edna H. Hong. Princeton: Princeton UP, 1992.
Saramago, José. *The Gospel According to Jesus Christ*, Trans. Giovanni Pontiero. New York: Harcourt Brace, 1994.
———. *The Tale of the Unknown Island*. Trans. Margaret Jull Costa. New York: Harcourt Brace, 1999.

MARK J.L. SABINE

"Once but no longer the prow of Europe": National Identity and Portuguese Destiny in José Saramago's The Stone Raft*

It seems paradoxical when a self-professed Marxist produces novels evincing deep scepticism about the viability of the "scientific" Marxist project of materialist historical analysis.[1] José Saramago and his fiction have presented such a paradox since *Baltasar and Blimunda* (*Memorial do Convento*, 1982), a paradox seemingly most acute in *The Stone Raft* (*A Jangada de Pedra*, 1986). Saramago's earlier novels merely questioned the accessibility of objective truth about the past. Yet the tale of an Iberian Peninsula sailing away from Europe not only denies the reader any explanation of the bizarre occurrences that it relates, but also seems to refute the possibility even of establishing a reliable approximation of the truth about the past. Moreover, the book's publication in the year of the Portuguese and Spanish states' commitment to membership of the EEC led many critics to interpret the forces that propel the fictional Iberia away from Europe as promoting not socialist internationalism but a form of separatist Iberian nationalism. Such an interpretation, however, fails to take account of two aspects of the text: first, its championing of the praxis of socialist revolution, and second, the full range of its postmodernist questioning of the nature of knowledge and historiography. While doubt is cast on the foundations of Marxist revolutionary theory, there are also clear indications at the novel's end that abandoning Europe is not in itself a solution to Spain's and Portugal's

From *Portuguese Literary & Cultural Studies 6. On Saramago* (Spring 2001). © 2001 University of Massachusetts Dartmouth.

problems. This study reads *The Stone Raft* as a text that, while conducting a postmodernist critique of the historiographical premises of Marxist revolutionary theory, simultaneously attempts to redirect the aims and values of Portuguese society away from the construction of a single European free trade zone and towards the construction of an egalitarian socialist society.

The Stone Raft is set in an immediate future bearing a close but hazy resemblance to the mid-1980s. In this imaginary temporal location, a deep crack opens up along the Pyrenees, and the Iberian Peninsula wrenches itself away from Europe and sails due west across the Atlantic, like a great stone ship or raft. After near-collision with the Azores, the Peninsula changes direction several times, following by turns a rectilinear, then a rotary trajectory before coming to an inconclusive halt between Africa and Latin America, roughly the heart of the post-colonial Hispanophone and Lusophone world. This inexplicable occurrence appears to coincide with five individuals' involvement in bizarre supernatural events. In Portugal, Joana Carda scratches an unerasable line in the earth with a stick of elm wood. José Anaiço is followed everywhere by a benign, yet otherwise Hitchcockian flock of starlings. Joaquim Sassa throws a huge rock into the sea, where it bounces over the waves until it disappears from sight. Over the border in Galicia, Maria Guavaira unravels an infinite length of blue yarn from an old sock, whilst elderly Andalusian Pedro Orce becomes a human seismometer, able to feel the earth trembling under his feet. Suspecting that their actions may have precipitated the geological aberration that has thrown their communities into turmoil, the five meet up and travel the floating landmass, seeking explanations to events in the seemingly exceptional objects and animals they encounter: the elm wand, the blue yarn, the starlings and a fearsome looking yet benign dog that leads them on a circular voyage around the Peninsula.

When the stone raft stops moving and the novel ends, the eldest of the five is dead, and the other four, now two couples and expecting parents, are left debating their futures. Their uncertainty about exactly how to continue their lives and love affairs is aggravated by the failure of their mission of discovery. Throughout the novel, a heterodiegetic narrative voice exposes the characters' conclusions about the determination of history as either implausible or unprovable, but also signals itself as the voice of an outsider who is by their own confession not only far from impartial but also wholly unreliable. This narrative voice gives conflicting evidence, points to lack of proof, or, when agreeing with the characters' suppositions, reveals its assessment of observed phenomena to be highly subjective by recounting events with absurd rhetorical overkill: hyperbole, pathetic fallacy, and speculation about the symbolic nature of an object or event. By highlighting the protagonists' ignorance of their exact circumstances and playing on the reader's desire to extrapolate clues to the Stone Raft's destiny from among the array of ambiguous symbolic referents, Saramago's text points to the abuse of rhetoric in humankind's attempts to interpret the unknowable, or at least indemonstrable truth about the past.

The belief that the full truth about the past is objectively irrecoverable suggests *The Stone Raft*'s authorial ideology to be closer to postmodernism than to Marxism. Through emphasis on the inevitable shortcomings of his/her account, the narrator demonstrates by example the inadequacy of even the purportedly most scientific accounts of history. It notes both the impossibility of collating all existing "evidence," or traces of the past—"the evidence relating to the period, the various documents, newspapers, films, video recordings, chronicles, private diaries, parchments, especially the palimpsests" (25)—and the impossibility of recovering data never committed to the record, as when it claims not to have been given all of the details of the story (203).[2] The narrative voice points to the selection of data for inclusion that anyone compiling an account of the past is obliged to make; the vast bulk of data that must be rejected by foreshortening an analysis of the geological makeup of the peninsula "because of the narrator's lack of knowledge and time" (23). By constantly interrupting itself with comments that satirise, contradict or retract data it has just asserted as, if not true, then at least worthy of the reader's attention, it indicates that the traces of the past frequently contradict one another, forcing the historian to judge which traces are more reliable and which tell more about the past. Inevitably, certain traces must be chosen over others, and some people's experience of the past must be privileged whilst that of others is ignored, as is demonstrated when the narrative voice vainly attempts to include the inhabitants of the peninsula that have been excluded from the story (91). As Keith Jenkins points out in *Re-thinking History* (1991), the traces of the past, whether written or archaeological, do not actually tell us anything; rather, they are the silent pieces of data that the historian manipulates in order to tell his/her own version of events (22 and 38). The subjectivity of the historian is inevitably brought to bear as traces are analysed, processed and codified to re-create the past. The historical account reflects the assumptions and opinions of the present day, and frequently the assumptions and opinions only of a socially privileged minority.

Postmodernist historiography questions the possibility of a single, unbiased account of the past and points out that accounts that are partial in both senses of the word are presented to us as concise and objective. As Linda

Hutcheon argues in *A Poetics of Postmodernism*, postmodernist narrative fiction has made a significant contribution to this critique of the assumptions of conventional historians and histories (105–12). Hutcheon uses the term "historiographical metafiction" for fictions that revisit the past to make satirical critiques of how the processing and codifying of images permits the construction of accounts of history in accordance with the dominant or "official" ideology of the present (5–6). Hutcheon's label fits perfectly for Saramago's two previous novels: *Baltasar and Blimunda* and *The Year of the Death of Ricardo Reis* (*O Ano da Morte de Ricardo Reis*, 1984). Both texts revisit key episodes of Portugal's past, drawing on data that official histories have ignored or suppressed—e.g., the experience of the peasantry and the proletariat—to create an alternative account that, while admitting its own ideological bias, asserts itself as no less valid than existing, equally ideologically motivated accounts. *The Stone Raft*, meanwhile, scrutinises the construction of the dominant conceptions of the present—1980s Portugal—and its ideological motivation: the project of EEC membership to which Saramago has repeatedly voiced his opposition. Helena Kaufman and José Ornelas, in their 1997 study of contemporary Portuguese fiction, observe how the official discourse of mid-1980s Portugal

> was already preparing the road for a union with the EEC countries, processing and codifying images which would rationalize its objectives. Even the future of Portugal was called into question; without the union there would be no future. Thus, an impression was created that the raison d'être of Portugal, the identity of its people, depended entirely on the formalization of the union. (162)

Primarily, *The Stone Raft* seeks to dismantle ideologies of EEC integration and to create a discursive space for a consideration of alternatives to EEC membership (Kaufman and Ornelas 162). The postulation of the Iberian Peninsula's inexplicable abandonment of Europe for an uncertain ultramarine destiny forms the premise for a chain of counterfactual events, which in turn facilitate the creation of a "counterdiscourse" of Portuguese identity and destiny. Interpolating the discourses of mass media, party politics and canonical literature, Saramago explores the construction and reinvention of national identity through the privileging, suppression and manipulation of both historical data and myth. The novel rearranges the building blocks of Portuguese identity formation—e.g., the nation's relationship to the oceans, the age of the Discoveries and of imperialist expansion eulogised by Portugal's national bard, Camões, and the literature of the purportedly unique Portuguese emotion of *saudade*—in order to suggest alternative inscriptions of a national ethos.

Although the novel does not assert a monolithic ideological program, it offers these alternative inscriptions as an argument for the viability of a political future for Portugal alternative to that of EEC membership: essentially, future action to eliminate social ills such as poverty, homelessness and sexual discrimination. It may seem hypocritical to denounce one political lobby's textual remaking of past and present as biased and deceptive whilst offering equally contrived, textual evidence to support an alternative agenda. Yet arguably any postmodern text must enter into this contradiction if it seeks to make an active intervention aimed at displacing the dominant ideology. I will argue that *The Stone Raft* effects just such an intervention through the self-consciously contradictory strategy of using counterfactual events to support a political message. It repeatedly advertises its inscription of Portuguese identity and destiny as just as much a rhetorical construction as the one it displaces, but in many instances the fiction that serves to provide justification of that inscription is based on an interpretation of genuine historical data: thinly disguised accounts of the authentic convulsion of Portugal's 1974 revolution. Saramago identifies a different national spirit at work in the social transformations of that period: an aborted project, the completion of which Saramago argues should be the national community's political priority.

The second half of this study explores how the novel treats the manifest practical problems in returning to such a project. As well as looking at what I consider to be the novel's contradictory approach to questions of nationality and identity, I aim to dispute readings by Mary L. Daniel, Piero Ceccucci and others who see *The Stone Raft*'s ending as the realisation of Utopia in an Iberia that has slipped the leash of capitalist Europe. Even in this counterfactual future, displacement to the mid-Atlantic can guarantee nothing more than a chance to rethink political options in relation to arguments inevitably based either on immaterial rhetorical devices or on subjective and selective accounts of history.

The novel charts how such subjective and selective histories fuel a debate as to whether or not Spain and Portugal are European. As the Pyrenean rift widens, "some member states came close to displaying a certain detachment, there is no more precise adjective, even going so far as to suggest that if the Iberian Peninsula wished to go away then let it go, the mistake was to have allowed it to come in" (31). Spain and Portugal's longstanding cultural engagement with neighbouring communities to the

north and east is conveniently disregarded in order to privilege the idea of
the two countries' status as newcomers, based on their only very recent entry
into western Europe's dominant political and commercial forum. But
opinion is sharply polarized: when the Peninsula does go its own way, a self-
styled movement of solidarity picks up across the continent, provoking
reaction in the assertion of an ideal European quintessence against which
Spain and Portugal can be measured and found wanting:

> Although it may not be very polite to say so, for certain
> Europeans, to see themselves rid of baffling Western nations,
> now sailing adrift on the ocean, from whence they should never
> have come, was in itself an improvement, the promise of happier
> times ahead, like with like, we have finally started to know what
> Europe is, unless there still remain some spurious fragments
> which will also break away sooner or later. Let us wager that
> ultimately we shall be reduced to a single nation, the quintessence
> of the European spirit, simple and perfect sublimation, Europe,
> that's to say, Switzerland. (125)

The irony is that the "nation" feted as "quintessential" is the one that
has most consistently declined to form alliances or join a European union.[3]
The so-called "Iberianist" lobby asserts the freedom of communities to
control their destiny free from outside influence when it declaims a slogan
echoing J.F. Kennedy's infamous "Ich bin ein Berliner": "We are Iberians
too."[4] The dream of a homogenous Europe, modeled on a society
inaccurately touted as a fusion of the politically and economically dominant
nations of the EEC is countered by an ideology of decentralisation and
cultural diversity. This ideology finds its fullest expression when the slogan
is scrawled on walls across Europe in seventeen languages, listed in full in the
text (126). This diversity, however, is served little better by the comfortingly
simplistic conception of a patchwork quilt of sovereign nation-states than by
a movement towards centralisation and homogenisation. The nation-states
that the political establishment eulogises as the "intrinsic foundations" of
Europe's identity are not organic entities but precarious constructs, "so
laboriously created throughout hundreds of years" (124). The Iberianists'
slogan and their protests convulse the continent precisely because they
question the integrity not only of the patchwork quilt but also that of the
component patches. The narrative voice's observation that the first
appearance of the graffito slogan—the French "Nous aussi sommes
ibériques"—could have been proclaimed first in Belgium or Luxembourg

(126) exposes what Benedict Anderson identifies as the fabrication of national consciousness through the arbitrary imposition of "print languages": standardised versions of vernacular dialects imposed as languages-of-state (67–80). As the protest gathers momentum, the phrase appears "in every conceivable language, even in regional dialects, in various forms of slang" (127) including, no doubt, the minority languages—Breton, Flemish, Alsatian, Occitan, Catalan, Basque—and dialects that French governments sought during so many years to eradicate yet which as spoken languages still extend across political borders, often merging indivisibly into one another.[5] Thus, the ethnic and cultural homogeneity of the nation-state is exposed as a mythical concept.

When European governments respond to the movement of "solidarity" with the Iberian peninsula by staging carefully rigged televised debates (127), the fragile artifice of *identidade europeia* is presented to the reader as a construction (or rather, a panicky reconstruction) in progress. Official media dictate the parameters of debates and impose a definition of opponents of European integration as "those restless spirits who unwisely ... put Europe's identity at risk" (164). Whilst in reality granting a platform only to those who will denounce the insubordination of a wayward, backward European periphery, these "debates" pay lip service to the tradition of free expression and democracy so frequently cited as a hallmark of that (western) European culture now imperilled by separatist fanatics.

This whitewash parallels that identified by Kaufman and Ornelas in the Portuguese media (162), which warned that opposition to EEC membership put the nation's future at risk. The novel also parodies media and government discourses in Spain and Portugal. In both countries an official interpretation of events on the shifting Portuguese coast is imposed through exploitation of two well-known yet conflicting inscriptions of Portuguese character: the Camonian image of heroic maritime pioneers and missionaries, and the image of a contemplative, fatalistic race abstracted in its collective sense of *saudade*, presented by the Spaniard Miguel de Unamuno in his *Por tierras de Portugal y de España* (*Through Portugal and Spain*) of 1910.[6] An embattled Portuguese prime minister apes Camões by assuring the people that the Peninsula's navigation—emphatically not a simple drift—makes Portugal the envy of Europeans who "see in this historic adventure into which we find ourselves launched the promise of a happier future, or to put it in a nutshell, the hope of regenerating humanity" (169). Meanwhile in Spain, television newscasters report Portuguese reactions to the peninsula's movement with a paraphrase of Unamuno's anthropomorphic portrait of Portugal as

a beautiful, gentle country girl sitting with her back to Europe at
the brink of the ocean ... resting her elbows on her knees and her
head between her hands, as she contemplates the sun's descent
into the infinite waters. (Unamuno 10)

The Spanish TV news is restricted to a single image of the coast,

with the waves beating on the rocks ... and lots of people
watching the horizon, with the tragic expression of someone who
has been prepared for centuries for the unknown.... There they
are now, just as Unamuno described, your dark face cupped
between both hands, eyes fixed on where the sun sleeps alone in
the infinite ocean. (*Jangada* 93; translation mine)

Further derision follows in the reference to the Iberian national
governments rejecting European protests "with manly pride on the part of
the Spanish and feminine haughtiness on the part of the Portuguese" (129).
This burlesque of Unamuno's sexist designation of Spain and Portugal as
respectively male and female dismisses the implication that Portugal should
behave like a good, subservient lady and agree to love and to cherish, to
honour and obey (Unamuno 10).[7] Appearances and commonplaces
regarding national character can, as Unamuno failed to realise, be
misleading: in Saramago's novel, ironically, it is the Spaniard Pedro Orce
who recognises in "the apparent melancholy of the city [of Lisbon] the
faithful image of his own intimate sadness" (83).

The reality—or at least that part of it experienced by the novel's
protagonists—does not match with these inscriptions. The lesson to be
learned is that it is easy to boast of unique specificities of national character,
but quite another thing to find proof for them: a nation's "nature of
conscience," if it exists at all, is plural, more amorphous and less distinctive
than many commentators would like to believe.

In addition to these parodies, the novel makes its own appropriations.
The echoes of the voyages of Discovery in the Peninsula's journey are
exploited in order to combat both European disdain for Portugal and native
nationalism. Portugal's primary role in the exporting of European languages,
religion and ideas, the importing of material riches of other continents and
related projects—from which stem many of the characteristics used to define
modern Europe—provides a substantial argument for the Portuguese
people's right to be considered European. At the same time, jingoistic
notions of Portugal's uniquely exalted status as instigator of ultramarine

exploration and conquest is debunked by revision of the bombastic Camonian epithet for Portugal: the prow or head of Europe. After the stone vessel turns 270 degrees on its axis, it sails south with Cap Creus in Catalunya, and not Cabo da Rocha in Portugal, as its prow (257). Elsewhere, however, the same epithet is called up to challenge Unamuno's view of the Portuguese. Portugal has ceased to be the prow of Europe not because its people are, as Unamuno asserted, exhausted and suicidal but because the country has sailed away from the European quay, as a ship of its own:

> Look at the Portuguese, all along their golden beaches, once but no longer the prow of Europe, for we have withdrawn from the European quayside to sail once more the Atlantic waves. (71)[8]

Saramago replaces these two chauvinistic inscriptions of national character with values of fraternity and pragmatism. However, he asserts these values as authentically Portuguese not by producing spurious, fictional examples, but by interpolating into the counterfactual sequence an event that parallels documented events of the revolutionary period. Just as in 1974–76 empty housing units in Portuguese cities were occupied by collectives of shantytown dwellers, so in *The Stone Raft* impoverished Algarve residents battle with police to take over abandoned hotel complexes and establish soviet-style communities.[9] The narrator sardonically recalls the Unamunian and Camonian models of Portuguese character:

> Seriously ... there are two different types of Portuguese, those who take themselves off to the beaches and sand dunes to contemplate the horizon despondently, and others who advance intrepidly on those hotels-cum-fortresses defended by the police. (75)

The old imperialist heroism gives way to a no more altruistic, but more egalitarian struggle to provide all of humanity with the basic necessities of life. This pragmatic egalitarianism informs the Portuguese people's spontaneous (if admittedly chaotic) evacuation of the coastal regions when it appears that the Peninsula is about to collide with the Azores. Saving their own skins whilst the Government of National Salvation dithers, the Portuguese confound Unamuno's expectations that they will wallow in the salt waters of their lachrymose "resigned desperation, or ... despairing resignation" (*Jangada* 17; translation mine) until the night of oblivion closes upon them.

However, in order to present this return to the values of 1974 the novel must contradict its own critique of the artificial boundaries drawn through communities by the state frontiers and print languages that, as Benedict Anderson asserts, serve as facilitators and guarantors of capitalist markets regulated by individual sovereign states (67–80). Saramago's splitting of the Pyrenees, creating an absolute division by deep blue water in place of the topographical semi-division of mountains, effectively legitimises the drawing of the boundary between citizens of two states whose only official print languages, until comparatively recently, were French and Castilian respectively. At the same time, it bisects the catchment areas of two dialect clusters that are today strongly affirmed as print languages by local populations: *Catalá* and *Euskera*. Indeed, students of separatist political movements within the Spanish state might argue that the most implausible thing about *The Stone Raft* is not that the Peninsula sails away, but that Catalonia and the Basque country do not split off and sail back to Europe. Analysis of *The Stone Raft's* treatment of Basque and Catalan nationalisms exposes narrative "silences" and "gaps" of the type that Marxist theorist Pierre Macherey famously identifies as pointing to the flaws and blind spots of a work's authorial ideology (85). Although *The Stone Raft* signals its consideration for the cultural concerns of Basque nationalism by, for example, calling Basque cities by their *Euskera* names—"Donostia," not "San Sebastián" (232) and "Gasteiz," not "Victoria" (224)—questions of Basque identity are effaced from the novel's first fifty pages, where the Pyrenean split is established. The split in the western Pyrenees appears in Orbaiceta, Navarra, and no Basque reactions are recorded. At the eastern, Catalan-speaking end of the range, cracks appear on both the French and the Spanish borders of Andorra before the tiny principality finally cleaves to the departing peninsula (23). No such apparent conflict of loyalties, however, is reported as the autonomous province of Catalunya breaks from Catalan-speaking Rousillon in France, while the Balearic islands—Catalan-speaking and politically united with Catalonia since the thirteenth century—disappear from the text altogether once it is reported that "so far there is no evidence that the islands have moved, but who can tell what tomorrow may bring" 29).[10] Reference to departure from the "European quayside" (71) casts Iberia in the role of one of Álvaro de Campos's "nation-vessels" [navios-nações], but the Iberian peninsula of the 1980s was surely a ship whose crew would sooner mutiny than accept the label of a single nation.[11]

Tensions between Spain and Portugal and their former colonies are similarly silenced. As the peninsula halts roughly equidistant from Puerto

Rico, Brazil and Guinea-Bissau, local reactions go unreported. The narrative seems coy about admitting that the Iberian nations, rather than physically assuming a position of privileged intermediacy between Europe and post-colonial southern America and Africa, need to initiate a mutually consensual, and thereby mutually beneficial, *rapprochement* with formerly colonised peoples as an alternative to accepting the weakening of ties dictated by EEC membership in the form of barriers on trade and immigration.[12] The reader of the novel should also note how the idea of an international movement in support of Iberia's separation from Europe can only be based on the dubious assumption of a pan-European stance of opposition to an expanded, integrated EEC. Many people who lived in, for example, Poland or Czechoslovakia during the 1980s would agree with Slawomir Mrożek and Milan Kundera that the real-life 1980s counterparts of the Polish *juventude* who write *My też jesteś my iberyjczykami* on the walls of Warsaw had a very different relationship to the idea of European identity from that either of Saramago's Portuguese or of their real-life counterparts. Mrożek and Kundera have both examined how their compatriots considered themselves to be Westerners and Europeans oppressed and isolated from Europe by a national power, Russia, which they, unlike Saramago (*The Stone Raft* 126), defined as non-European, or as belonging to a separate, Eastern Europe.[13]

While Saramago's Poles seem to express only the aspirations of the Portuguese, in the novel there is one voice outside Iberia that is allotted the opportunity to speak on behalf of its own interests: that of the US president. Though the narrative hints that the roving Peninsula may have surprises in store for the directors of the capitalist world order (255–58), that world order is still in control at the novel's end. Contrary to what is suggested by Daniel's and Ceccucci's emphasis on portents of positive social change in *The Stone Raft*, at the novel's end the transformation of Portuguese society remains unguaranteed.[14] Since the occupation of the Algarve hotels, there has been no clear evidence of social change. Just as the ideals of 25 de Abril had become increasingly confounded or compromised in the Portugal of the 1980s—the occupations of empty housing blocks, for example, being ruled unlawful and evictions being forced following legislation passed in April 1975—so in *The Stone Raft* processes that intimate social change are derailed or discredited.[15] The "Iberianist" solidarity movement collapses into violence and chaos, an echo of the lack of organization and pragmatism that arguably characterized many popular movements of the late 1960s and early 1970s. Meanwhile, Portugal's incoming Government of National Salvation is exposed as simply a cynical repackaging of the incumbent governmental team, whose fecklessness is revealed when catastrophic collision with the

Azores threatens. Although the collision never occurs, the Portuguese government suffers the humiliation of being overruled by its US counterpart—the supreme power of international capitalism—when it attempts to monitor the situation on its own sovereign territory (189).[16]

Changes of greater profundity are initiated more adroitly by the novel's five protagonists, whose journey around the Peninsula creates new social conditions and conventions, in particular new freedoms for the two women to control their own destinies and to engage in acts of love without surrendering their liberty. Joana Carda tells her three male companions that she went to Lisbon in search of them "because I saw you as people detached from the apparent logic of the world, and that's precisely how I feel myself to be" (*Jangada* 147; translation mine). Just as the logic of natural physics is defied by the movement of the Peninsula, so the social logic of western civilisation is challenged, as conditions on the road and under canvas dictate a new and less sexist division of labor. When, for example, the five turn to peddling clothes in Spain for a living, each individual contributes according to his/her talents and training. The two women select stock, the accounting is handled by Joaquim Sassa, and the Spanish-speaking dispensing pharmacist Pedro Orce handles the sales patter whilst Portuguese-speaking José Anaiço stays back at the wagon preparing food (205–08).

Perhaps more significantly, when Maria Guavaira and Joana Carda freely admit to having had sex with Pedro Orce, it becomes clear that their new way of living means new practices of loving. Both women are determined to reject the notion that a lover is physically and spiritually the property of his/her partner, and assert that if their partners cannot understand their position, then the journey, the friendships and love affairs are all invalid and must end. When Joana Carda invokes the elm wand to support the assertion of her and Maria Guavaira's guiltlessness, she reminds her companions that for her the wand is still the totem of her freedom, the rod with which she marked her independence in the soil at Ereira and which "can still be used to draw another line here" in order to determine "who is to remain on this side and who on the other" (229): the demarcation of a new beginning and new social rules.[17] Joana Carda's relationship to the elm wand constitutes a great temptation to conjecture that the use of the elm tree as a symbol of dignity in Western Christian iconography could have relevance here, suggesting the dignity that for millennia has been denied to women while their bodies are controlled and traded by fathers and husbands.[18]

But while the two women are both "making exception the rule" in order to create more propitious rules (240), there is no reason to believe that these changes reflect transformations in society as a whole. Joaquim Sassa makes the comparison between the five friends' lifestyle and that of gypsies (202). Like gypsies, they inhabit the social and economic margins, and their lifestyle remains different whilst the rest of society recovers from the threat of collision with the Azores ("people are returning to their normal habits and pursuits, if that is the right word to describe their former habits and pursuits" [244]). On the day after meeting her new friends, Maria Guavaira rejects the privations of widowhood by substituting her old, colorful clothes for dark mourning dress. But although the flamboyant garments that she and Joana Carda hang out to air "billow and flutter like flags," and although "one feels like shouting Long live liberty" (155), there is no confirmation that shouting or flying flags will change anything. By the end of the novel, Joana Carda's cousin is presumably still "casada e mal-maridada"—married to a bad husband—in Ereira (*Jangada* 158), and, presumably, she is also pregnant.

The impregnation, shortly before the end of the novel, of the entire population of fertile women on the Peninsula throws a very big spanner into the engines of this tentative, unfinished movement towards female liberation. Critics such as Ceccucci have interpreted the mass pregnancy as a positive symbol, as the "total redemption through love" that predicates "the ascent of a new class of humanity; of a new epoch not merely hoped for and dreamed of, but also willed and constructed" (214). For two reasons, however, one must take issue with this optimism. First, unplanned pregnancy *en masse* would not universally be deemed a blessing in 1980s Portugal, given the country's long history of criminalisation of abortion and the Estado Novo's use of a cult of large families as a means to keep women in the home and out of public life.[19] Secondly, the occurrence leaves the novel and its protagonists literally in a state of expectation. The birth of Joana Carda's and Maria Guavaira's children will be the acid test of their relationships and the new rules of partnership, division of domestic labor and now paternity that they have negotiated. Furthermore, the enigma of the two foetuses' paternity, and the uncertainty as to where and by whom the children will be raised, make it impossible to guess what cultural and national or regional loyalties they will develop, or what influence they and their 12–15 million as yet unborn contemporaries will have on social organisation on the Iberian Peninsula of the future. The allegory of the peninsula's geopolitical realignment, and the new paradigms of national and gender identity, provide tentative suggestions for the future, but cannot guarantee Utopia any more than Iberia's "rebirth" can be proven by a poet comparing the rotating peninsula to a baby turning in the womb (252).

On the last page of the novel, Pedro Orce is laid to rest, the narrative voice is silenced, and fundamental and unanswered questions resonate in the air: "who knows what future awaits ... how much time, what destiny" (263).

As a rainy day dawns, prospects are not much brighter for the four remaining protagonists than for the Iberianist opponents of US and EEC intervention. Neither of the two couples is completely reconciled following discussion of the paternity of the unborn children, and there is no certainty as to what they will do with their lives now that they have no dog to guide them. Will they perpetuate their journey and the new values of communality and sexual equality, or will they dissolve their ad-hoc marriages and resume their former existences? The only intimations of social change are the wholly ambivalent symbols of renewal: the unborn children, the fanciful image of the peninsula as an unborn baby, and the green but budless elm wand that Joana Carda plants on Pedro Orce's grave. The elm branch, previously possessing ambiguous resonances of a magic wand, a symbol of a wife's declaration of independence, a lucky charm, might sprout and grow to become a Tree of Life, symbol of hope and regeneration, or a broad and spreading elm, symbolic of a woman's realized independence and recognized dignity. Then again, it might not. The parallel drawn between Pedro Orce's burial and that deemed suitable for the exiled Spanish poet Antonio Machado (56 and 260) not only reopens discussion of the problematic relationship between territory and identity, but also warns against excessive optimism by highlighting the reference, on the novel's final page, to Machado's poem "A un olmo seco" ("To a dying elm-tree") in *Campos de Castilla* (Machado 799–800).[20] Machado's poem addresses a rotting, half-dead tree whose single green branch makes the poet long for "another miracle of the Spring."[21] By association with this the elm branch stuck in the barren desert of Venta Micena comes to represent not the certainty of a future Utopia but the precarious nature of human hopes and aspirations. It may develop into a "resuscitated tree," but only "if a piece of wood stuck in the ground is capable of working miracles" (263).[22] Unamuno implied that the Portuguese have been ill-served by their faith in miracles.[23] *The Stone Raft*'s inconclusive and unpromising ending argues that, even when the reassuring certainties of materialist analysis of history prove ill-founded, life, and the struggle to make life better and fairer, must go on. The only certainty, in Portugal, Spain or elsewhere, is that the actions of the common people must be added to the rhetoric of politicians and novelists, if a better society is to be built out of a humanity fragmented by economic, ethnic and generic divisions.

NOTES

*The author would like very gratefully to acknowledge the invaluable contribution of Dr. Hilary Owen, of the University of Manchester, in reading, commenting on, and where appropriate, querying aspects of several successive drafts of this article.

1. Interviewed, in 1986, by Clara Ferreira Alves, Francisco Bélard and Augusto M. Seabra for the *Expresso* magazine supplement in "A facilidade de set ibérico" ("The Simplicity of Being Iberian"), Saramago reaffirmed his commitment to Marxism and to "a materialist view of the world" (Saramago 1986).

2. All quotations from *The Stone Raft*, except where otherwise indicated, are from Giovanni Pontiero's translation. All other translations of quoted material are my own.

3. Switzerland has been neutral since 1815. In a referendum in 1993, following the creation of a European Economic Area that the Swiss government was compelled to join, the Swiss electorate rejected ratification of an agreement to enter the European Community (*New Encyclopaedia Britannica*, XXVIII.355).

4. Kennedy's actual words were: "All free men, wherever they may live, are citizens of Berlin, and therefore, as a free man, I take pride in the words 'Ich bin ein Berliner'" (qtd. in Schlesinger Jr. 808–09).

5. Adrian Battye and Marie-Anne Hintze identify the Revolution of 1789 as the catalyst for "the crystallisation of a feeling that the dialects and the minority languages spoken on the French national territory constituted some kind of external threat" (41). Abbé Grégoire's *Rapport sur la nécessité d'ánéantir les patois et d'universaliser l'usage de la langue française* (Treatise on the Necessity of Annihilating Primitive Speech Forms and of Universalizing the Use of the French Language) of 1794 formed the basis for a state primary education policy with the principal objective of imposing what, 127 years later, the *Bulletin officiel de l'instruction publique* (*Official Bulletin on Public Education*) of 1921 termed "the language of Racine or Voltaire" in place of the urban slang ... the village patter ... the regional dialect" (Battye and Hintze 42 and 48). The teaching of such "dialects" as Basque, Catalan, Breton and Occitan in French state schools was outlawed until 1951, that of Corsican until 1974 and that of Flemish until 1976. By the mid-1970s, Basque, Breton and Corsican separatist political parties were still outlawed in France and many of their leaders still imprisoned (Gordon 100–02).

6. Unamuno talks of two facets of the Portuguese *ethos* as represented in Guerra Junqueiro's poems *Os Simples* (*The Unaffected*) and *Pátria* (*Fatherland*): "the bucolic Portugal, impassive and unaffected ... and ... the heroic, noble Portugal" (19). In the same book, his observations on contemporary Portugal indicate that for him the latter facet is an attitude restricted to, or lost in, the Portuguese past: Unamuno compares the Portuguese to Ulysses who "returned to domesticity and ... ensconced by the hearth, contemplating the rise and fall of the flames, which call to mind the crests and troughs of the ocean waves, would recount to his children and grandchildren tales from the thick of battle and from his far-flung expeditions" (21). It should be noted that *The Stone Raft's* Camonian references have no truck with the connection made by the organs of the Estado Novo—in works such as José Leitão de Barros's epic film *Camões* (Lisboa Filme, 1946)—between Camões, the calumniated hero who dies awaiting the return of days of Imperial glory, and the fatalistic cult of *Sebastianismo*.

7. In one passage Unamuno compares Portugal to the hapless Inés de Castro (91).

8. See Unamuno on Portuguese fatalism (38–39) and suicidal tendencies: "Portugal is a nation of suicides, perhaps, indeed, a suicidal nation" (80). He also quotes Camões (*Os Lusiadas* X.145) in talking of "the sea, which was once Portugal's glory, the sea, which has granted her immortality in the history of humankind, the sea has delivered her 'into the clutches of lusting greed and into the brutishness of a harsh, gloomy and detestable

sadness' ['no gosto da cobiça e na rudeza / d'huma austera apagada e vil tristeza']"
(Unamuno 48–49).

9. Two detailed contemporary accounts of the post-revolutionary housing struggles
are Downs and Ponte. *The Stone Raft* also recalls the collapse of the Portuguese tourist
industry that accompanied the period of unrest in 1974–75 (Maxwell 141), and the
subsequent use of empty Algarve hotels to accommodate not the local homeless, but some
of the 500,000 *retornados* from the former "overseas provinces" in Africa. This initiative
must have provoked resentment among the indigenous population, and almost bankrupted
the post-revolutionary Portuguese state. Concern for the welfare of the *retornados* did not,
however, extend to allowing them to stay on in the hotels once tourists could be coaxed
back (Morrison 51–52).

10. The Balearic islands were conquered by Jaume I of Aragón by 1235. Together with
Catalonia they were ruled directly by the Aragonese monarchs, apart from a period of
autonomous monarchic rule on the islands from 1298–1349 ("Balearic Islands," in *New
Encyclopaedia Brttannica*, 15th ed. [1995], 830).

11. Campos (Fernando Pessoa), "Ode Marítima," stanza 9, line 1: "Ah, the Great
Quay from which we embark in Vessel-Nations! [Ah o Grande Cais donde partimos em
Navios-Nações!]" (Pessoa 136).

12. Saramago advances the following argument regarding Portuguese and Spanish
relations with former colonial communities:

> I admit that, for the right or wrong reasons, those whom we once set out to
> find may want to forget who we are but, if I might be permitted the
> indulgence of prophecy, I foresee that we will end up finding our own
> cultural vitality diminished if we persist in seeking or accepting solutions and
> goals which, through our own erroneous conception of them as exclusive of
> other solutions and goals, might lead us to ourselves forget who we are. ("A
> Peninsula" 11)

13. Mrożek, interviewed by Timothy Garton Ash, identifies a belief widespread
amongst educated Poles that they, "unlike the Russians, indubitably belong" to Europe
and to "the West" (Mrożek 97). Kundera (in 1980) makes a distinction between two quite
separate European civilizations:

> As a concept of cultural history, Eastern Europe is Russia, with its quite
> specific history anchored in the Byzantine world. Bohemia, Poland,
> Hungary, just like Austria, have never been part of Eastern Europe. From the
> very beginning they have taken part in the great adventure of Western
> civilisation ... The post-war annexation of Central Europe ... by Russian
> civilisation caused Western culture to lose its vital centre of gravity ... and we
> cannot dismiss the possibility that the end of Central Europe marked the
> beginning of the end for Europe as a whole. (230)

14. Daniel writes of the "promise for a brighter future of continued life on the new
continent" in a novel that expresses an "optimistic and robust vein of confidence in the
future" (541), while Ceccucci refers to "a new era hoped for and dreamed of, but also
willed and established" (214).

15. According to Charles Downs, the earliest enforcement of the 17 April 1975 Anti-occupation Decree was in January 1976 (*Commissões de moradores* 20–23). Due to considerable popular opposition, it was not until 1978 that evictions took place on a large scale.

16. This episode can be interpreted as another reference to events following 25 April 1974, specifically the intervention of the USA in Portuguese affairs, motivated by concern about the future of its air base at Lajes in the Azores. Only two months after the coup, President Richard Nixon met General Spínola for private talks about Lajes and Portugal's membership in NATO. The US Secretary of State, Henry Kissinger, apparently favoured subjecting Portugal to total isolation in order to suffocate any attempts at revolution (Morrison 26–28).

17. Joana Carda's gesture recalls a passage in Saramago's *Levantado do Chão*. Here, a line scratched in the earth challenges abusive husband Domingos Mau-Tempo's claim to hold authority over his wife, Sara da Conceição, who has taken refuge along with her children in the home of her kinsman José Picanço:

> With his staff, Domingos Mau-Tempo scratches the earth in front of him, to all appearances it's a challenge, the signal for a brawl, and Picanço interprets it that way, and makes himself prepared, grasping hold of a stick.... Behind him, on the other side of the door, are three terrified children and a woman who would fight to the death to protect them if she could, but the two sides are badly-matched, and so Picanço takes a chance and etches his own scratch in the earth. (48–49)
>
> Whereas Sara da Conceição, living in the Alentejo circa 1910, must rely on male relatives to protect her from her husband, Joana Carda determines not to be dependent on any man.

18. The association of the elm tree with dignity is discussed by Roig (69).

19. Following legislation in 1984, abortion is legal in Portugal only in certain extenuating circumstances. Prior to 1984, abortion was expressly banned in any circumstances. However, in the period immediately prior to 25 April 1974, an estimated 200,000 illegal, and often very unprofessional, abortions were carried out annually. These resulted each year in around 2,000 recorded fatalities (Salgado 8). In 1936, Salazar's Estado Novo established OMEN (Obra das Mães para a Educação Nacional), aiming to "bring up the 'new woman' from infancy to be a good Catholic and patriot, and in the future a 'prolific' mother and an obedient wife" (Rosas and Brito 609 and 675). These groups organized annual "Mothers' Weeks" from 1938 until the 1960s, and "attempted, by means of hand-outs of cribs, hope chests and prizes for 'prolific' mothers, to combat restrictions on the index of population growth and ... to promote the return of women to domesticity" (Rows and Brito 676).

20. Significantly, Pedro Orce drops dead outside the hermitage of Turruchel, just south of Bienservida, at the border between Castilla La Mancha and his native *autonomía* of Andalucía (259). Pedro Orce's earlier declaration that "my [native] land is Andalusia," and that other parts of the Spanish state such as Galicia mean nothing to him because "it's possible for us not to know our own state, but we all know our own land" (*Jangada* 178; translation mine), can be interpreted as an attempt to distinguish between a chauvinistic, nationalist cult of *o país* ("the state") and a more benign sentimental attachment to *a terra* ("the land").

21. The passage in *The Stone Raft* does not quote any poem from *Campos de Castilla* but

echoes the association Machado asserts between his soul and the landscape of Soria in, for example, "Campos de Soria" IX, lines 1–8:

> Yes! You travel with me, Sorian fields....
> You have found your way into my soul,
> or perhaps you were always rooted in its depths? (772)

and in "Caminos," lines 41–46:

> There, in the highlands—
> where the Duero traces
> its crossbow curve
> around Soria, amid lead-coloured hills
> and the smudges of ragged oak groves
> my heart is wandering in dreams (804).

The author would like very gratefully to acknowledge the assistance of Mr. David McLoghlin in his translations from Machado's work.

22. The planting of the elm on Pedro Orce's grave also recalls the miracle of St. Zenobio, recounted in Eça de Queirós's *Dicionário de Milagres* (174). On its way to burial, the coffin of Bishop (later Saint) Zenobio of Florence accidentally struck a dead elm tree, which burst immediately into leaf. Pedro Orce, it would appear, is no St. Zenobio.

23. "Deep down, we Spanish have less faith in miracles.... We do not believe in the return of a King Sebastian" (Unamuno 40).

WORKS CITED

Anderson, Benedict. *Imagined Communities: Reflections on the origin and spread of nationalism.* 2nd ed. Revised and extended. London: Verso, 1991.

Battye, Adrian, and Marie-Anne Hintze. *The French Language Today.* London: Routledge, 1992.

Camões. Dir. *José Leitão de Barros.* Lisboa Filme, 1946.

Ceccucci, Pedro. "L'Utopia Saramaghiana come Progetto della Storia Umana." *Il Girador Studi di Litterature iberiche e iberoamericane offerti a Giuseppe Bellini.* Ed. G.B. De Cesare and Silvana Serafin. Rome: Bulzoni, 1993. 209–15.

Daniel, Mary L. "Symbolism and Synchronicity in José Saramago's *A Jangada de Pedra.*" *Hispania* 74.3 (Sept. 1991): 536–41.

Downs, Charles. *Commissões de Moradores and Urban Struggles in Revolutionary Portugal.* Unpublished, c. 1979. No. 220, 332.34 Dow. Arquivo do Centro de Documentação do 25 de Abril, Universidade de Coimbra.

Gordon, David C. *The French Language and National Identity, 1930–1975.* The Hague: Mouton, 1978.

Hutcheon, Linda. *A Poetics of Postmodernism.* London: Routledge, 1988.

Jenkins, Keith. *Re-thinking History.* London: Routledge, 1991.

Kaufman, Helena, and José Ornelas. "Challenging the Past/Theorizing History: Postrevolutionary Portuguese Fiction." *After the Revolution: Twenty Years of Portuguese Literature 1974–1994*. Ed. Helena Kaufman and Anna Klobucka. Lewisburg: Bucknell UP, 1997. 145–67.

Kundera, Milan. *The Book of Laughter and Forgetting*. Afterword by Kundera and Philip Roth. Trans. Henry Michael Heim. London: Penguin, 1980.

Machado, Manuel and Antonio. *Obras Completas*. Ed. Heliodoro Carpintero. Madrid: Plenitud, 1967.

Macherey, Pierre. *A Theory of Literary Production*. Trans. Geoffrey Wall. London: Routledge and Kegan Paul, 1978.

Maxwell, Kenneth. *The Making of Portuguese Democracy*. Cambridge: Cambridge UP, 1995.

Morrison, Rodney. *Portugal: Revolutionary Change in an Open Economy*. Boston: Auburn House, 1981.

Mroźek, Slawomir. Interview. "Under Eastern Eyes." *Granta* 20 (Winter 1986): 89–104.

New Encyclopedia Britannica. 15th ed. Chicago: Encyclopedia Britannica, 1995.

Pessoa, Fernando. *Poesias de Álvaro de Campos*. São Paulo: FTD, 1992.

Ponte, Bruno da. *Housing Struggles in Portugal*. Unpublished, c. 1975–76. No. 167, 333.32 Pon. Arquivo do Centro de Documentação do 25 de Abril, Universidade de Coimbra.

Queirós, Eça de. *Dicionário de Milagres*. *Obras Completas*. Lisboa: Livros do Brasil, s.d.

Roig, J. Fernando. *Simbología Cristiana*. Barcelona: Juan Flors, 1958.

Rosas, Fernando, and J.M. Brandão de Brito, eds. *Dicionário de Historia do Estado Novo*. 2nd vol. Venda Nova: Bertrand, 1996.

Salgado, Abílio José. *A Situação da Mulher na Sociedade Portuguesa Actual: Os preconceitos e a luta pela emancipação*. Lisboa: Iniciativas Editoriais, 1978.

Saramago, José. Entrevista. "A facilidade de ser ibérico." *Revista Expresso* 8 Nov. 1986: 36–39.

———. *Levantado do Chão*. Lisboa: Caminho, 1982.

———. "A Península Ibérica entre a Europa e a América Latina." *Vértice* 47 (Mar.–Abr. 1992): 5–11.

———. *The Stone Raft*. Trans. Giovanni Pontiero. London: Harvill, 1995. [Trans. of *A Jangada de Pedra*. Lisboa: Caminho, 1986.]

Schlesinger Jr., Arthur Meier. *A Thousand Days: John Fitzgerald Kennedy in the White House*. London: Mayflower, 1967.

Unamuno, Miguel de. *Por tierras de Portugal y de España*. Madrid: España-Calpe, 1941.

RONALD W. SOUSA

José Saramago "Revises," Or
Out of Africa and Into Cyber-History

Nobel Prize winner José Saramago's most cited novels are complexly allusive to Portuguese culture. Everything from official history and canonized literature to historical documentation, local histories, urban planning, and many strands of contemporary popular culture, both national and international are invoked, in jumbled and a-chronistic fashion, in such titles as *Memorial do Convento* (1982) (English trans.: *Baltasar and Blimunda*). It is probably because of that mode of presentation—and the irreverent tone that accompanies it—that while Saramago sells extremely well in Portugal and the rest of the Portuguese-speaking world and has become so well-known internationally that the Nobel Prize for literature has followed, he is not held in high regard by a significant portion of the Portuguese literary and intellectual establishment. His long-standing public adherence to the Portuguese Communist Party doubtlessly adds to that low regard which perhaps in turn underpins his preference to make his home in neighboring, and rival, Spain.

Another way of characterizing Saramago's practice is to observe that rather than focus on a discrete set of issues, as conventional novelistics dictates, his novels regularly mix discourses, cutting across a broad swath within the Portuguese symbolic, explicating, critiquing, interrelating, and intervening, apparently at whim, as they go—and clearly, in the process,

From *Discourse*, vol. 22, no. 3 (Fall 2000). © 2001 Wayne State University Press.

claiming a considerable operativity for themselves within that symbolic realm. This practice is most in evidence in his "historical" novels, the aforementioned *Memorial do Convento* and both *O Ano da Morte de Ricardo Reis* (1984) (*The Year of the Death of Ricardo Reis*) and *A História do Cerco de Lisboa* (1989) (*History of the Siege of Lisbon*), which take on a labyrinthine character as a result. Indeed, in *O Ano da Morte de Ricardo Reis*, the image of the labyrinth is thematized and played upon. This essay intends to explore such aspects of that diffuse but simultaneously blatant operativity as touch on the Portuguese colonialist imaginary.

It is a truism in Portuguese cultural criticism to observe that over the past two decades the nation has been, and continues to be, interrogated and symbolically reconstructed through reference to the twin poles of national history and colonialism—because those were key areas within which the inherited concept of the nation was principally constructed. Less regularly mentioned is the fact that (as the ensuing pages will evidence) national history and colonialism come so interwoven that reconstruction often has to be directed to both at once. It will not, therefore, surprise that, in order to explore issues having to do with the colonialist imaginary, these pages will focus on a "historical" novel—at first glance, an unlikely one for the purpose—*História do Cerco de Lisboa*, which deals not with a colonial subject matter but instead with the Christian taking of Lisbon from the Arabs in 1147. Or, rather, it deals with the complex interaction between that past event and an obscure present-day Lisbon copyeditor named Raimundo Silva.

Early on, *História* takes on a form that the Portuguese reading public would find quite recognizable: it involves a central character who is also an author writing an historical text by drawing on a prior historical text for his material. Alluded to—in effect an intertext to *História*—is the novel *A Ilustre Casa de Ramires* (*The Illustrious House of Ramires*) (1900) by the classic realist novelist Eça de Queirós (1845–1900). A standard of Portuguese literature, *Ilustre Casa* gives us one of its most fascinating and problematic figures: the hereditary nobleman Gonçalo Mendes Ramires. In Saramago's *História*, Gonçalo is clearly enough alluded to that not far into the book he becomes an ongoing "pair" of Raimundo Silva. Their life situations are similar, their plot location in many ways identical, and *História* continues to produce textual echoes, when not what are essentially parallel passages (cf., e.g., *História*, 318 [285] and *Ilustre Casa*, 59 [51]), all of which keep that doubling before the reader. The result is a specific configuration of the textual labyrinth, namely the palimpsest. It is as though *História* were written over *Ilustre Casa*, with the latter still showing through in multiple places and exercising a continual but irregular modelling power over the more recent novel's situations and narrative trajectory. As regards reader reception, that palimpsest serves to present over and over again the points of contrast between aspects of *História* and the classic realist text.

Gonçalo Mendes Ramires of *Ilustre Casa* has it as his principal activity to explore his family past—which is set up as analogous to Portuguese national history—through his writing of a new historical text about some of his ancestors. He does so by using—one might more appropriately say "plagiarizing"—a text on the same subject written by one of his more recent forebears. One aspect of the interest generated by the past/present confrontation is that through it Gonçalo is ultimately able to identify and knowingly break out of the stifling sociability patterns presented throughout Queirós's prior work as characteristic of the Portuguese society of his time (*Ilustre Casa* was published in the year of its author's death). The set of issues that Queirós invokes have to do with the project (institutional or putative) of installing a version of socio-cultural modernity[1] in the country—of replacing what *Ilustre Casa* calls the circular "a-history" (348, 350 [297, 300]) characteristic of Portuguese society with linear "history."

Although Gonçalo's "escape" is problematic and interpretation continues to be debated, its final step is clear: he goes to Africa, to the future Mozambique, to accomplish something on his own—precisely to leave "a-history" and enter "history." It is a rehearsal of the late-nineteenth- and early-twentieth-century Portuguese imperialist impulse, carried out during the time of the Treaty of Berlin (1884–1885), and subsequent European "scramble for Africa," in which Portugal was a significant player. The escape itself is prepared for in an internal dialogue that Gonçalo carries on with his family past through the vehicle of his writing project. The basic pattern that the dialogue takes on is that of the "talking cure": when the subject is able to articulate a clear, exteriorized picture of the problem (in this case, when Gonçalo is able to fashion a critical outlook upon his family/national heritage), a self-activating reason comes to the fore and works to overcome the identified problems, emancipating itself in the process. The activity that confirms this particular version of such emancipation is one that has been projected out of Portugal and onto Africa.

That projection displays a number of features characteristic of the modern Portuguese colonial outlook. At its core, there lies the controlling metaphor that colonialism is the self-expression of an essential "Portugueseness" rather than, say, a primarily economic undertaking or the advent of something to be seen as culturally *sui generis*. Viewed as the self-expression of Portugueseness, colonialism envisioned Africa as a space upon which the national problematic could be projected, expressed, and even worked on. A part of that outlook had it, in effect, that there was no content in Africa itself. *Ilustre Casa* is especially revealing in this regard in the easy conflation—if not equation—that it simply presumes of prospective modernity in Portugal and colonialism by Portugal. That conflation comes grounded in the presumption of the absence of any African content that might intervene and create different conditions for metropolitan modernity and colonial activity. What Gonçalo apparently does in Africa (we are told, not shown) is precisely indicative of that conflation. He replays the hierarchical social relations that have both characterized his own life and also provided the basis for Portuguese colonialism, as well as the accompanying colonialist agricultural (indeed monocultural) practices: he becomes a planter of coconut, cacao, and rubber trees (355 [304]). In short, his practice is one that, in its overall outline, is merely characteristic of European colonialism. Within the logic of the novel, however, that activity (perhaps sarcastically[2]) is equated to the achieving of modernity. That modernity is characterized— by Gonçalo himself—as follows:

> ... thinkers complet[ing] their explanations of the universe; artists achiev[ing] works of eternal beauty; reformers perfect[ing] social harmony; saints improv[ing] souls in saintly fashion; physiologists lessen[ing] human suffering; inventors increas[ing] the wealth of nations; magnificent explorers wrestling] worlds from sterility and silence. (344 [294])

Too the novel presents the colonial as an emanation of national history: in his world, Gonçalo's choice to go to Africa exists as a logical consequence of his linking up of past and present in critical fashion, thus leaving colonialism-seen-as-modernity to function as the paradigmatic future. At the same time, it is telling that modernity-seen-through-colonialism can be achieved only in a scenario symbolically less proximate to what is understood to be cultural modernity than Portugal itself, as though, for Portugal, modernity can come into being not in relation to models of modernity but only in relation to something even-less-modern and only in a secluded space.

Thus is produced the picture of a putative modernity that is configured in the imaginary as a schematized desire. At the moment it is subjected to symbolization, however, it must stay very general (e.g., Gonçalo's analogic approach in the passage reproduced above), and projections and exclusions must be created for it (e.g., the absence of actual Africans) in order that it be sustainable. This internally contradictory set of impulses doubtless expresses in its own way the set of contradictions within which Portugal has existed. It has long functioned as an economic dependency of northern Europe (and, more recently, the United States)—in world systems terminology, a "semi-peripheral area" (see Hopkins and Wallerstein)—while simultaneously remaining an old-style colonial power into the mid-1970s and gaining a measure of economic stabilization from that position.

The fascist regime that held power in the country from the early 1930s up to the 1974 revolution thematized this internal contradiction and sought to legitimate it in the following terms: the colonies (by the 1950s they were called "overseas provinces") are "spiritually" a part of Portugal; Portugueseness is capable of producing and sustaining the only positive European colonizing; Portuguese colonial space is therefore unique and uniquely positive, and the rest of the world, along with dissidents at home, in their criticism only reveal that they do not understand Portugueseness. The Portugal-centeredness of this outlook is made clear in the argument, often advanced by the regime in defense of its continued colonialism in times of European decolonization, that the "abuses" overseas—even the Colonial Wars themselves—were "accidents" (in, virtually, the Scholastic sense of the term) that should not be seen to detract from the "essential" positiveness of Portuguese colonialism. Such statements, again, amount to admission of the presumption that the only "real" content in Portuguese colonial space is Portugal-originated rather than local. Those tenets anchored a cultural *isolat* that gradually grew throughout the period from the end of World War II to 1974, until it became the dominant theme of state discourse on national identity. Moreover, as a part of that *isolat*, a highly-identificatory mode of reception of cultural products was posited (and institutionalized in educational practice) that presumed receiver recognition of Portugueseness as a hermeneutic first step in understanding. A corollary of that position was that therefore understanding of Portuguese culture was open only to "real" Portuguese (Sousa, "Pessoa Literary Criticism," 216–219).

In sum, the Portuguese colonial imaginary, to which *Ilustre Casa* contributed in its own time and has continued to contribute through reading and (re-)interpretation thereafter, has it that the colonies represent the necessary presence through which Portugal can become modern. Simultaneously, however, that modernity, by the very nature of its supposed core features—its self-actuation and reflexivity—must necessarily be achieved by Portugal acting solely upon itself. Clearly, the two conditions are irreconcilable. That divergence has long represented a key problem within the Portuguese cultural symbolic.

Saramago's *História do Cerco de Lisboa* revisits these issues in multiple ways. The novel itself is centered on a short period in Raimundo Silva's life as he works as a contract copyeditor for a large Lisbon publishing house. One day he is given a book to edit entitled *A História do Cerco de Lisboa*. It is a book of history about that key moment in consecrated Portuguese history, an event and date that every Portuguese schoolchild memorizes in the same way that an American schoolchild memorizes 1775 and the battles of Lexington and Concord. Now, for reasons not wholly clear but having to do with, among other factors, middle-age crisis, free-floating disaffection, and intellectual arrogance (he is intellectually offended at the book's jingoistic combination of presumption of impossible knowledge and accompanying historical inaccuracies), Raimundo takes it into his head to subvert if not history then at least historiography. Historically speaking (or so we are told), the taking of Lisbon was decisively aided by a large number of crusaders, principally Norman, Flemish, and English, who had stopped in Lisbon before proceeding on to the Holy Land to fight in the Second Crusade. Raimundo, when it comes to the relevant passage in the book he is copyediting, chooses to add the word "*não*," thereby producing the statement that the crusaders decided *not* to aid the proto-Portuguese in their quest to take Lisbon.

From this perverse addition—or, perhaps, this perverse subtraction— all else in the *História* flows. The title becomes, then, multiply ambivalent: a novel title that repeats the title of a book on a traditional subject in the process of being undone in the novel itself. By dint of his "*não*" Raimundo ends up being called to the attention of his (female) editor, with whom he ends up establishing an intimate relationship built on his iconoclasm. As a part of that relationship the editor, Maria Sara, actually challenges Raimundo to write a "history" of the siege of Lisbon presuming his negation, his "not," and all that it brings with it.

Thus in ways extremely similar to *A Ilustre Casa de Ramires* the reader is presented with a main character who is the author writing a historical text (of sorts) based on a prior text (of sorts) upon which other texts bear in specific ways. As in the Queirós novel, what is presented, then, is a network of texts representing the character/author's (and the Portuguese reader's) "national" heritage. Also as in the earlier novel, the reader is given verbatim extended passages of the historical text-under-construction as— presumably—it passes through the mind of the character/author and out onto the page. Thus are we able to see how history is used and reused, how the historical imagination works. In the interface between heritage and present that the two novels have in common, their palimpsestically profiled differences come to the fore.

The text of *Ilustre Casa* establishes a history of ancestral vigor that

Gonçalo has to meet in his own terms to enter modernity. By contrast, Raimundo has set for himself an almost logical problem: much like Descartes demonstrating the function of "doubt," he has to show in his new version of the siege of Lisbon how it might have been possible for the Christians to take the city even without the aid of the crusaders. Let me hasten to reassure you, in case, as a bearer of Western culture, you were worried, that after considerable trial and error, on both the Christians' part and Raimundo's, a way is found and Lisbon is still taken. The contrast, however, reveals that in many respects Raimundo is the inverse of Gonçalo: the inherited national history is, in the former's novelistic reconstruction, merely a set of rhetorical and logical possibilities, not, as it was for Gonçalo, a cultural or family inheritance, not a force, psychological or ethnic, in some manner to be identified with, transformed into present terms, and projected as a part of the colonialist exportation of "Portugueseness" necessary for Portugal to "progress" culturally. When history is looked at as Raimundo Silva is forced, by the logic of his project, to look at it, many questions about the nature and function of historiography are posed and set in motion. (It is important to note that in Portuguese "copyeditor" is "revisor"—literally "re-viser" or "re-seer." Suggestions of "making over"/"seeing afresh" abound in the novel.)

It is quite clear as Raimundo and Maria Sara conceive the project and he begins to carry it out, that at stake are what are appropriately understood as a set of probabilities: Raimundo has to ask himself how Lisbon can still be taken without the manpower and military expertise that the crusaders represent. He literally has to calculate military odds and plan strategy. He is able to do so by walking where he lives and looking over what was the actual terrain of the siege of 850 years earlier or by looking out from his terrace—palimpsestically paired with the "Ramires Tower," from which Gonçalo can similarly look out over the scenario of past events about which he is writing. Raimundo comes to think of that scene as a large chessboard (233–234 [207]). By now it is clear that, despite his unremarkable character, there is a sense in which Raimundo is aptly named: in this specific cognitive sense, in relation to these specific sorts of operations, he is the "king of the world," albeit a world of his own creation. In (re-)writing history he becomes King Afonso Henriques, Mem Rodrigues, and other Portuguese historical personages. Indeed, the novel dedicates a great deal of time to analysis of how he "becomes" such figures. The controlling metaphor for that process is one that can best be called "cyber-historical"—in very specific ways.

At first glance, the linking of something that might be called "cyber-history," or "cyber"-anything, and a Portuguese novel would seem to be nonsensical. Portugal is hardly the home of advanced computer culture; no

Neuromancers have yet come out of Lisboa or Porto, or seem poised to do so any time soon—though the narrative voice of *História* tantalizes us with several short meditations about computers (26 [18], 248 [221]). Yet on its very surface the novel has something to do with phenomena otherwise linked to role-playing games and MUD's.

Throughout the historical portion of *História* one sees a process of calculation of the strengths and leadership abilities of personages in a world principled by rules according to which the probabilities of success or failure of possible operations are analyzed, much as in role-playing games. We also see psychological projection, identification, and the like on the part of Raimundo become the narrative and rhetorical gestures necessary for getting Lisbon "still taken." Rather, then, than chess, Raimundo is in fact playing something like the classic "Dungeons and Dragons" or today's on-line "Ultima." As a result, his negation of inherited historiography has the effect not of replacing one "story" with another but rather of moving the writing of history away from a "modern" model characterizing it as controlled by a self-actuating and self-sufficient reason, with the product of which one can identify (which is Eça de Queirós's view and a conceptualization with which Gonçalo Mendes Ramires literally seeks to join in order to enter modernity) and to a model based on video-game-like structures of interactivity and changing realities.

That modal shift is so much the case that, out of the many personages that inherited history offers him, Raimundo quite openly chooses a "character" to "play." What that means in game culture is, first and foremost, that the game-player creates—or co-creates with others—the game world according to rules that he or she must subsequently obey in playing the game and that he or she then has an effect within that world through the actions of a "character" or "characters" in that world with whom he/she identifies to some extent and in some ways. The usual means of describing this effect in the world of the game is to say "I want to do this," or "I expect that," etc., in which the pronoun "I" is a combination of the player and the character but represents the character's motives within the game world. Lest there be doubt that Raimundo's choice of "his character" involves a process like this, let me show you a relevant passage:

> A Raimundo Silva, a quem sobretudo importa *defender, o melhor que souber*, a heterodoxa tese de se terem recusado os cruzados a ajudar à conquista de Lisboa, tanto lhe fará uma personagem como outra. ... No moço Mogueime atraiu-o a desenvoltura, se não mesmo o brilho, com que relatou o episódio [da tomada de

Santarém]. ... Aceita portanto Raimundo Silva a Mogueime para
sua personagem, mas considera que alguns pontos hão-de ser
previamente esclarecidos para que não restem mal-entendidos
que possam vir a prejudicar, mais tarde. ... (189–190; emphasis
mine)

[As for Raimundo Silva, whose main concern is *to defend as best
he can* the unorthodox theory that the crusaders refused to take
part in the conquest of Lisbon, he will be satisfied with one
character as with another. ... He was drawn more by young
Mogueime's lack of inhibition than his powers of narration as he
listened to his account of the attack on Santarém. ... Therefore
Raimundo Silva assumes Mogueime as his character, but believes
certain points ought to be clarified beforehand, so that there will
be no misunderstandings that might later prejudice. ... (168)][3]

In the last lines of that passage Mogueime's "powers" are being established,
as when a character is created in role-playing games and given so many
"points" for strength, for cleverness, etc. It is clear that Mogueime is being
chosen as Raimundo's "character" in exactly the sense that MUDders and D
and D players use the term.

It takes little foresight to imagine that our combination of
Raimundo/Mogueime will come up with a love interest within their
combination of history/game world—her name is Ouroana. Nor does it take
foresight to imagine that that phenomenon will represent a cyber-pairing
with Raimundo and Maria Sara. Indeed, such is the case to the point that the
developing narrative (in which Maria Sara reads along as Raimundo writes)
structures their lovemaking and their developing relationship and, inversely,
their lovemaking and relationship become a source of material and motives
for the eventual Crusader-less conquest of Lisbon. For example, Raimundo
conspicuously kills off a Germanic knight in order to open the way for the
relationship between Mogueime and Ouroana to develop (282–319
[251–286]), in a blatant transferential relationship to his own developing
intimacy with Maria Sara. In general terms, neither realm, the contemporary
"reality" or the history/game regularly occupies a master role: they model
each other interchangeably, decision-making in one leading to decision-
making in the other. Indeed, this interchangeability operates to the point
where, by the end of *História*, virtually any event taking place in one world
serves as a metaphor, implicit when not explicit, for something in the other.

Saramago's novel, then, "cybernizes" Portuguese history through the
suggestion that that history can be received and organized in any number of

potential ways and that those alternative organizations owe as much to the receiver/organizer and his or her circumstances as to the content. It is as though the novel were seeking to intercept the highly identificatory hermeneutics advanced under fascism and turn it 180 degrees. Instead of a reading that urges unproblematic identification with characters on the basis of shared nationality, *História* sets one forth that literally complexifies the process by instantiating a reader–character relationship that, cybernetically, admits the rhetorical value of identification but at the same time suggests that the identification should be one in which the reader role is self-consciously developed and understood. In effect, the reader should read in such a way that s/he reflects on the reader-function as a part of carrying it out. The past, *História* suggests, should not be received as though it were given somewhere and had a powerful fixing relationship with the receiver. It should be received as a bundle of information variably narratizable and differentially meaningful across whatever diversity describes the receivership and, conversely, its formative impact on the receiver should be recognized in reception. The contrast with *Ilustre Casa de Ramires* functions to put that suggestion in strong relief: Gonçalo's strategy involves the mere re-definition of the terms in a static relationship with a constituted history, while Raimundo's is based on a present-time-oriented mutability within the terms of that relationship. Moreover, in Saramago's work that emphasis on mutability is not limited to the area of plot. A very specific, albeit implicit, pact is built with the reader in, especially, the "historical" novels. Those novels work in a manner I have called "heuristic" (Sousa, "Saramago ..."), achieving a part of their reader-implied author relationship by opening up narratively a space for review of the grand history that had been set up as the centerpiece of the "official" hermeneutics. In effect, the narrator/implied author continually whispers to the reader something like: "you and I have been told all our lives to see this this way; let's instead see what happens if we try to see it entirely differently. This is my way at this moment." In effect, what is created is a reader/author space both for shared irreverence and for celebration of the role that such irreverence plays in the reading of the novel. "Cyber-history" stands as an extended metaphor for that process.

One of the fascinating things about cyber-technology is its multiple interrogation of subjecthood. The relationship between computer-generated worlds and narration has been studied by Janet Murray (1997), their implication for subject constitution by Sherry Turkle (1995), both of MIT. What *História* does with Raimundo Silva, and, in parallel manner, with its own readership, has parallels to findings scattered through those studies. It simultaneously models and exercises the proposition that subjecthood can be less fixed and less monocular than has been presumed to be the case both in classical theories of subjecthood and—importantly for present purposes—in the identificatory hermeneutics promoted by Portuguese fascism: that potentially we can hold more than one world fully in our minds at once and be flexible enough to relate fully to both or all of the possibilities involved.

As should be expected, the question of the colonial comes as part and parcel of this review of history. It comes to the fore in several different passages or sequences of passages. The first—which seems a self-conscious satire of *Ilustre Casa*—involves emphasis upon the highly romanticized Eurocentric view of Africa in which the inherited colonialist concept is grounded. Within the logic of *Ilustre Casa* Gonçalo chooses to go to Africa for his "escape" because of a long-ago reading of H. Rider Haggard's *King Solomon's Mines* (89 [76–77]), a novel that Eça de Queirós actually translated into Portuguese (*As Minas de Salomão*). That fanciful romanticizing of Africa—and accompanying emptying of it of contemporary content—is doubled in *História* when Raimundo goes into a reverie about Tarzan and a lion, in a free association with a children's book he once read (79–87 [68–76]). Haggard is thus slyly replaced with Edgar Rice Burroughs, and the romantic is satirized through its trivializing exaggeration.

Second, early in the historical portion of the text, Raimundo observes that over time many people have judged the proto-Portuguese besiegers of Lisbon to be the lesser of the two combatants in terms of cultural achievement. He chooses specific terminology: "cafres rematados, regalados na sua testarrudez," ("out-and-out rustics who rejoiced in their stubbornness") (64–65 [55]). "Cafre," translated as "rustic," is roughly the English "kaffir," though in Portuguese it is both used generically to refer to sub-Saharan African peoples and also to mean "devoid of culture," "primitive," or simply "stupid." The inversion of the stereotypes underpinning colonialism is obvious, as is the implicit reminder that the defending Arabs—the "other side" in the "besieger/besieged" equation to which "kaffir" comes appended—are themselves in the main an Africa-derived people. But such implications are not what is important; what is important is the obviousness of the selection of that particular, unlikely adjective in that particular context. In effect, then, the principal point being made is that a point is being made.

A third, and highly complex, set of allusions come as the siege of Lisbon, as Raimundo re-writes it, nears its successful outcome. Several aspects of the invaders' culture are referred—not without immediate comic effect—to Portugal's colonial wars of the 1960s and early 1970s, the resultant Revolution that overthrew the fascist regime in 1974, and their aftermath.

While it is nowhere textualized, the understood irony is that the 1974 Revolution, planned principally in Guinea, was carried out as an Africa-to-Portugal operation, that, in a curious way, the colonies' ignored content ended up overthrowing the metropole. It is not that the allusions to the colonial wars (e.g., 284 [254], 338 [302–302]) and to the Revolution (340 [305]) establish any sort of counter-narrative to the colonialist position. It is rather that they—along with the other thematizations of Africa in the text—suggest that there has been all along a relationship with Africa other than one merely of projection upon it from Portugal and that that relationship has involved very tangible matters, not some abstract logic of ideal and accident. In the wider terms of the colonialist imaginary, it involves the suggestions that Africa's absent presence has represented a conceptual error within the Portuguese imaginary; that that error has had very tangible historical ramifications that the grand history, by its very logic, was unable to see; and that that conceptualization can be superseded by re-vision.

In sum, this novel about an event in 1147 manages to define, undercut, and redirect an entire set of culturally ingrained assertions about colonialism, all the while seeing that issue as one within a larger set of issues having to do with the entirety of the inherited national culture. It is not that Lisbon is not "still taken" in Raimundo Silva's version of the siege. It is rather that his conceptualization of the taking is one in which the receiver is asked to organize him- or herself in such a way as both to identify with the matters being represented, albeit in a conditional manner, and at the same time to be aware of a "free space" in which matters can be rethought and/or rearranged, all as a part of the very process of reception. The "free space," which has been characterized above as one reserved for review of the paradigms of inherited culture, also has more basic dimensions to it. Within the logic of *História*, it is the space of the historical imagination psychologized: Raimundo's motives for choosing certain routes to the taking of Lisbon overtly reflect his own subject position. The suggestion, of course, is that this is an integral, though heretofore occulted, part of the historical imagination. It is also the space in which subjecthood is constituted. What *História* posits in its recourse to the game model is a subjecthood very different from the classical modern one to which Gonçalo Mendes Ramires aspires. It is one that trades not on modern-style identificatory processes but rather on examination of alternative realities through an identification that remains conditional. Such an outlook coincides in some important ways with Richard Rorty's contention in effect that at this point in the development of Western culture we can leave off with uniform transcendent "realities" and work on the basis of recognized intersubjectivity and consensus-building (1–34). The ultimate implication of *História* in its operation as re-viser of the Portuguese national symbolic as regards colonialism is that a subject constituted in relation to such logic as Rorty outlines has no need of the hidden presence of an empty "Africa" as a vehicle for its own self-maintenance.

In sum, the operativity that *História do Cerco de Lisboa* claims for itself is a wide and daring one. In that sense, it is indicative of the current disposition of Portuguese thought and of the gravitation that José Saramago has sought within it. *História* presumes its reader's experience with the grand national history and with the expectations in the area of hermeneutics that, under fascism, came with that grand history. Using those elements as a point simultaneously of departure and of comparison, it explores not so much specific alternatives as the nature that such alternatives might assume. In the process it also explores implications that might ensue in the area of subject-constitution in relation to narration of nation and reception of such narration in a moment when, for the first time in the modern era, "Portugal" cannot be defined, overtly or covertly, in relation to a colonial presence.

NOTES

1. Here and throughout I refer to what has been the operating sign of the concept "modernity" over the past two centuries, namely Enlightenment modernity. As is well known, it stands as distinct from "early modernity." For a discussion of that distinction, see Mignolo, 55–60.

2. As I have remarked above, *Ilustre Casa*'s ending is problematic. It is therefore variously read. It is quite defensible to read it as widely ironic and to interpret the tone as one of a sarcasm that suggests the improbability of the escape. For present purposes, however, what is relevant is the novel's overall pattern—i.e., the terms in which the escape is couched—not any specific reading of its last pages, and that pattern is accurately characterized here. The only reading of the novel that might complicate my argument is one that would see *Ilustre Casa* as satirizing the very notion of seeing colonialism as modernity—in which case it would pointing out what, in the terms of n. 1 above, would be a category error consisting of Gonçalo's aiming for Enlightenment modernity but being able to conceptualize it only in the terms of early modernity. Such a reading would not seem to find support elsewhere in Queirós's work. To my knowledge, this is the first time it has been suggested.

3. The "game" connection is clear in the Portuguese. The English translator apparently did not see that connection, or chose not to render it, and as a result, the translation partially obfuscates it.

WORKS CITED

Eça de Queirós, J.M. de. *A Ilustre Casa de Ramires*. 6th ed. Lisboa: Livros do Brasil, n.d.

———. *The Illustrious House of Ramires*. Trans. Ann Stevens. Athens, Ohio: Ohio UP, 1968.

————— *As Minas de Salomão*. Lisboa: Livros do Brasil, n.d.

Hopkins, Terence K. and Immanuel Wallerstein. *World-Systems Analysis: Theory and Methodology*. Beverly Hills: Sage, 1982.

Mignolo, Walter D. *Local Histories/Global Designs: Coloniality, Subaltern Knowledge, and Border Thinking*. Princeton, NJ: Princeton UP, 2000.

Murray, Janet H. *Hamlet on the Holodeck: The Future of Narrative in Cyberspace*. New York: Free Press, 1997.

Rorty, Richard. *Objectivity, Relativism, and Truth: Philosophical Papers, Volume 1*. Cambridge: Cambridge UP, 1991.

Saramago, José. *O Ano da Morte de Ricardo Reis*. Lisboa: Caminho, 1984.

—————. *Baltasar and Blimunda*. Trans. Giovanni Pontiero. New York: Ballantine, 1987.

—————. *História do Cerco de Lisboa*. Lisboa: Caminho, 1989.

—————. *History of the Siege of Lisbon*. Trans. Giovanni Pontiero. San Diego: Harvest, 1996.

—————. *Memorial do Convento*. Lisboa: Caminho, 1982.

—————. *The Year of the Death of Ricardo Reis*. Trans. Giovanni Pontiero. New York: Harcourt Brace Jovanovich, 1991.

Sousa, Ronald W. "Pessoa Literary Criticism and the Antagonistic Literary Institutionality of the Estado Novo." *Indiana Journal of Hispanic Literatures* 9 (Fall 1996): 211–224.

—————. "Saramago, His Readership, and the Modalities of History,—or Dragging Their Telos Behind Him." Lisboa: Caminho, forthcoming.

Turkle, Sherry. *Life on the Screen: Identity in the Age of the Internet*. New York: Touchstone, 1995.

—————. *The Second Self: Computers and the Human Spirit*. New York: Simon and Schuster, 1984.

PAULO DE MEDEIROS

Invitation to the Voyage

> Tout y parlerait
> A lame en secret
> Sa douce langue
> natale

The last twenty years have seen a, perhaps unprecedented, surge in Portuguese literature. Already extremely rich, Portuguese literature after the revolution of April 25, 1974, has been dynamized by the appearance of a number of great writers. The last quarter of this century, far from indicating decline, as one could expect from its millenary quality, will be marked by the impetus brought on by varied writers, some of them present here today, who have renewed Portuguese literature and made it one of the most vibrant in the West. Instead of becoming lost in a morass of post-modern complexities or post-colonial complexes, current Portuguese literature, without losing track of such transnational phenomena, has been charting new spaces for the questioning of national identity and contributing towards the constant process of redefinition of humanity. Straddling literary generations, José Saramago has become one of the most important, and most recognized, Portuguese authors, whose international projection has contributed to form an idea of the contemporary literary scene in Portugal. Novels such as *Memorial do Convento* (1982), or *A Jangada de Pedra* (1986), have had a wide

---

From *Global Impact of the Portuguese Language*. © 2001 by Transaction Publishers.

audience in Portugal and abroad, and have contributed to a renewed attention to Portugal, not merely as a favorite vacation destination or the once weak member of the European Union, but rather as a complex society whose deep roots in history no longer serve to tie it into a morbid fascination with the past. Indeed, Portugal's long history can be seen now as ground for its projection into the future, a future imagined in its literature, which is being shaped, individually and collectively, in conflict and in cooperation with the international community.

After the final dissolution of empire, and the reintegration into a European political arena, Portugal has had to question its role. Letting go of the myths fostered, and at times imposed, by the propaganda of the "Estado Novo," which had kept Portugal tied to an illusory past, made only of great deeds and away from the realities of the twentieth century, the Portuguese have had to accept their semi-peripheral position in the world system, as Boaventura de Sousa Santos has demonstrated.[1] At once the holder of vast colonies in Africa and to a great extent colonized culturally and economically by France and the United Kingdom, Portugal was a suspended anachronism. If the Salazar regime had forced an image of Portugal standing alone against all, certain of its historical greatness, and imagining that fighting a devastating colonial war was the inevitable expression of its national destiny, the effect was almost its opposite. Immobilized by the awe its historical feats provoked and by the resentment of no longer occupying that position in the world, for many Portuguese, Portugal became rather a sign of shame, the Portuguese language a prison rather than a home, and only what was foreign was appreciated. Certainly these sentiments did not originate in 1928 and have other roots. Yet, the blinds forced on the Portuguese nation by the dictatorship greatly intensified and generalized them. One of the achievements, not the only one, but one of the most important, of contemporary Portuguese literature, is the partial reversal of such fatalistic notions. By this I do not mean at all that recent Portuguese literature has embarked on a simple celebration of being Portuguese. Instead, it has been through a sometimes merciless reexamination and criticism of Portuguese history and society that current literature has been able to redirect and reshape the image of Portugal. There is still much to be done, of course, but two decades after the revolution the innovative force of Portuguese letters has already done much to give the Portuguese new and different reasons to identify with and to be proud of their name.[2] What this implies, though, is that if in many cases contemporary Portuguese literature has directly engaged the national question, it has both served as a catalyst for, and necessitated, a rediscovery of Portugal by all, and foremost by the

Portuguese. A nation of travelers, the Portuguese, for the most part, had always directed their sights outwards, to the seas, either in search of new worlds, or, more recently, simply in search of the minimal means for a dignified existence, which the brave new world of Salazar forced them to seek through immigration and exile. The time has come, and has been coming for long, to turn one's gaze inland, to try to see Portugal as it is, to discover in that process a nation and a people, whose name, Portugal, should be invoked not in vainglorious fits of isolationist nationalism, but with the natural pride of recognition for the human achievement that it represents. This process of search is what José Saramago's book, *Viagem a Portugal*, initiates, and its reading is an invitation to us all, Portuguese or not, to start such a voyage.[3]

All of Saramago's works can be said to be marked by the sign of travel, as several critics have remarked, and the author himself seems to be in continuous motion. A novel such as *A Jangada de Pedra* perhaps best exemplifies the importance of travel in Saramago's imagery, as not only are its main characters in constant travel through Spain and Portugal, but the whole of the Iberian peninsula itself is in motion after its separation from the continent, until it comes to rest, at least temporarily, in the middle of the Atlantic in triangulation with America and Africa. As such, the Iberian peninsula becomes a trope of tropes, a metaphor for travel, and itself a traveling metaphor of the nation, imagined not along political lines but cultural ones. Critical attention has focused on the novels, and these perhaps constitute the author's most lasting achievement, or at least the one with the wider impact. Saramago, however, has been active in all genres, from poetry to drama, including the short essay or chronicle, and from these *Viagem a Portugal* clearly stands out by its scope and theme. The book has been completely ignored by critics, and yet in it one finds not only a work of literary achievement but also a document that clearly speaks of Portugal in a way that it would be difficult to find duplicated anywhere else, and to which one well could apply the words from Baudelaire's famous poem cited in the epigraph, "Tout y parlerait / A l'âme en secret! Sa douce langue natale," for this is a book in which not only does one hear the love for the Portuguese language that distinguishes all of Saramago's writing, but especially, what one can read in all the pages of this book is precisely the way in which it speaks of Portugal and its spirit. This is not the nationalist and populist spirit of the nation invented by demagogues for their own consumption and to blind the people, but rather the spirit of the land and of the people who have lived in it for centuries and for whose achievements, whose lives, Saramago searches. Through his search these achievements are revealed for all of us, and we are invited, in turn, to initiate such a search for ourselves.

The dedication that opens the book is a double marker, directed as it is to those without whose collaboration Saramago's travel could not have been done, those whose keys literally opened the doors to the innumerable churches scattered throughout the country, whose ignored works of art Saramago describes, and also to the one literary precursor, Almeida Garrett who, without really having written a book of travels in Portugal, wrote the book of travels in Portugal, *Viagens na minha terra*, a novel generally acclaimed as a masterpiece and as a mark of the modern period. The appropriateness of the dedication becomes even clearer once one considers how, metaphorically, the "opening of doors" is also an opening into a questioning of the image of Portugal one has and how, by writing a factual narrative of travel into which stories are continuously interwoven (be they traditional legends, imagined episodes, or the descriptions of the encounters the narrator experiences), Saramago has indeed invoked and inverted Garrett's model. To start examining the book, I would like to consider the way in which it is framed, that is, how its opening and closing sequences provoke reflection into the very nature of the narrative, of travel, and of travel narratives.

The short preface is used by Saramago to spell out certain key aspects of genre, starting with the affirmation that his book is not a guide or travelogue and that, although full of personal opinions, these are not meant as advice (13). Such an admonition is further emphasized at the end of the preface by another in which the author hopes the readers will take the book as an example and not as a model, whereby the differentiation is crucial not because of any false modesty, which is not intended, but rather by the fine distinction Saramago makes and in which is implied his desire not to construct a controlling, totalizing narrative but rather one that is open and that should make possible further inquiry. In the preface Saramago also fuses travel and narrative, indicating how in his perspective (and in this literary tradition certainly bears him out), writing is also always a trope for travel, and the two are indissociable.[4] This is how Saramago expresses it:

> Esta viagem a Portugal é uma história. História de um viajante no interior da viagem que fez, história de uma viagem que em si transportou um viajante, história da viagem e viajante reunidos em uma procurada fusão daquele que vê e daquilo que é visto. O viajante viajou no seu país, isto significa que viajou por dentro de si mesmo, pela cultura que o formou e está formando, significa que foi, por muitas semanas, um espelho reflector das imagens exteriores, uma vidraça transparente que luzes e sombras

atravessaram, uma placa sensível que registou, em trânsito e em processo, as impressões, as vozes, o murmúrio infindável de um povo. (13–14)

These affirmations are not quite unproblematic and, in effect, they already reveal precisely to what extent Saramago's project in this book succeeds towards a re-evaluation of Portugal in general, and towards the more particularized goal of inscribing himself into a neglected literary tradition. The affirmations also reveal to what extent Saramago's project still conceals some of the problems inherent in such an attempt. By classifying his narrative as a story Saramago is not merely defending himself against any claims of lack of objectivity, or proclaiming the evident subjective nature of the experiences narrated, but also and foremost claiming for his text a literary quality and inserting it into a genre and a tradition. Furthermore, by asserting that the narrative is a story not only of a voyage but of a traveler, indeed of the internal voyage of a traveler, Saramago is explicitly calling the reader's attention to the way in which the narrative, at the same time that it is constructed by the author, also constructs a certain subjectivity. I am not referring to the need to distinguish between the figure of Saramago, the author, and the narrator, which in a book of this nature is as hard as it is necessary to maintain, but rather to the fact that Saramago, who throughout uses the term "traveler" to refer to the narrator in third person, far from pretending thus to establish an air of objectivity, wants to reinforce the very fact that subjects are themselves always constructed through their own narratives. Besides, Saramago's claims also call into question, indeed attempt to dissolve, any neat separation between outside and inside, object and subject. If the narrative constructs a vision of reality, that is of Portugal, which can be said to be really there, it is also a very partial narrative, constantly framed and filtered through an individual consciousness that, in turn, is constantly being shaped itself by the very nature of the reality encountered. This might seem a simple game, and yet it is also crucial for an understanding of why Saramago asked that his book be taken as an example and not as a model, why he, in effect, does not claim to present more than a perspective on Portugal which, if in its richness does serve to represent to many a hidden facet of the nation, cannot be confused with a representation of the nation.

One problem that the preface raises has to do with the claims of transparency. Saramago uses three images to refer to the process of his travels when he says that, for many weeks, he was a reflecting mirror, a transparent glass, and a film that registered "the impressions, the voices, the endless murmur of a people." The first two metaphors are very traditional, and the third one might have been motivated in part by the fact that in its original form the book contains many beautiful pictures of the places Saramago visited, the people he met, and the objects he described. Had Saramago used only the first two images, his position of conflating the borders between inner subjectivity and outer reality would have been, if not denied, at least seriously compromised. Yet, the third metaphor, even if it does not manage to completely disperse the problems raised by the first two, does complicate them and comes closer to bearing out Saramago's initial claim. More problematic than the image of a reflecting mirror is the image of a transparent glass through which, supposedly, the reality of Portugal can be represented, can speak out. It would seem to propel Saramago's position into an unwanted totalization. However, if one superimposes all three images and tries to imagine that the glass, rather than being transparent, is in between the film already sensitized by the external images and the external images themselves, one can approximate Saramago's position previously enunciated. That such a sandwiching is not without difficulties becomes evident in the narrative itself, for as much as Saramago offers a critique of representation, he also cannot completely avoid it. Before turning to that question, however, I still want to pursue the issue of borders.

If, in the preface, the borders invoked only to be dissolved are those between inside and outside, the real and the imagined, the subject and the object of consciousness, the very beginning of the narrative in itself posits another questioning of borders, this time focused on the geographical and political borders. This is the opening scene narrated by Saramago:

> De memória de guarda da fronteira, nunca tal se viu. Este é o primeiro viajante que no meio do caminho pára o automóvel, tem o motor já em Portugal, mas não o depósito da gasolina, que ainda está em Espanha, e ele próprio assoma ao parapeito naquele exacto centímetro por onde passa a invisível linha da fronteira. Então, sobre as águas escuras e profundas, entre as altas escarpas que vão dobrando os ecos, ouve-se a voz do viajante, pregando aos peixes do rio. (15)

The fact that Saramago thus inaugurates his narrative as an allegory at the same time that he inscribes himself in the figure of Saint Anthony, only to radically redirect the sermon towards a message against the falsity of nationalisms, is itself significant. But what is striking is the fact that Saramago, by doing so, also conditions his narrative in several ways. First, by deciding to start his voyage through the north of the country, Saramago could be said to approximate, in a sense, historical developments as Portugal expanded southwards. Yet, he also carefully avoids inscribing himself into any original narrative, as he does not start with the putative birth of nationality, Guimarães. At the same time, Saramago also de-centers his narrative by not starting from Lisbon, for long his place of residence before he went to Lanzarote. Indeed, Lisbon will also be one of the places visited, but in no way does it constitute a center or place of origin. By starting his travels from Spain, Saramago already gives an alternative perspective to the whole of the narrative, since in order to initiate his travels in his country he decides to do so from another country. And, at the same time, by creating the scene where his initial motion is temporarily suspended in the precise but imaginary liminal space of the frontier between the two countries, Saramago, in effect, not only questions the very existence of borders but also calls for their relativization. The sermon he delivers to the fish, praising them precisely for ignoring such artificial boundaries, is humorous, but in the following chapters there is a constant preoccupation with examining what life on the border might be and the realization that, in spite of imposed political barriers people, not unlike fish, also pay more attention to family bonds and ties of affinity than to national borders.

Towards the end of the narrative, there is this same questioning of borders. Traveling towards Elvas, Saramago consults a large, detailed military map and notices that, in the vicinity of Olivença, it omits the border between Portugal and Spain:

> ... o viajante. ... repara que na carta militar que lhe serve de melhor guia não está reconhecida como tal a fronteira face a Olivença. Não há sequer fronteira. Para norte da ribeira de Olivença, para sul da ribeira de Táliga, ambas do outro lado do Guadiana, a fronteira é marcada com uma faixa vermelha tracejada: entre os dois cursos de água, é como se a terra portuguesa se prolongasse para além do sinuoso traço azul do rio. O viajante é patriota. Sempre ouviu dizer que Olivença nos foi abusivamente sonegada. ... Se os serviços cartográficos do Exército tão provativamente mostram que Portugal, em trinta ou quarenta quilómetros, não tem fronteira, então está aberto o caminho para a reconquista, nenhum tracejado nos impede de invadir a espanha e tomar o que nos pertence. (340)

The irony that suffuses this passage, as well as the decision announced by Saramago to pronounce himself publicly in favor of annexing, or reintegrating Olivença to the national space, does not leave room for doubts as to the position of the author on the nature of national borders, even if less clear than the initial sermon to the fish. More importantly, however, and perhaps more forcefully than in the beginning (where the reader is asked to imagine the traveler in the absurd situation of preaching to the fish while going through customs), this passage calls attention precisely to the fictional nature of national borders. The lack of a border between Portugal and Spain in the area of Olivença does not simply denote the obstinacy of the Portuguese government in holding on to a historical claim—or the impossibility of the same government acting on its territorial claim, irregardless of the feelings of the local population—but rather the fact that maps, besides being objects to facilitate travel, are also foremost tools for the construction of national identity. The lack of a border in this case, on a Portuguese military map, does not indicate that the sermon to the fish has been accepted and the Portuguese can imagine themselves to be not too different from their neighbors, but rather its opposite—that the government could hypothetically invoke such an absence precisely to invade the neighbors.

The question of the map also raises another issue that is fundamental towards an appreciation of Saramago's project, and that is the question of representation. For the map, after all, is a visual representation of the territory said to be national and, in a way, Saramago's narrative is also, although differently, a representation of the same territory or, more precisely, of the way in which people have been living in that territory, which artistic record they have left of themselves and, as such, also a representation of what future can be imagined. Saramago starts by questioning the validity of representation, as I have noted, even if he still slips into traditional notions of representation as transparency. Indeed, it is such a slippage that is interesting. Throughout the narrative Saramago has occasion to repeatedly question the validity of verbal representation. The following passage gives an example in which, after listing a series of places he has not visited, Saramago notes:

> O viajante viu estes casos pelo mapa, não lhe impõe o seu roteiro que por todos aqueles lugares passe, mas tendo notado a abundância, mal parecia que não registasse. Lástima tem o viajante de que uma linha de palavras não seja uma corrente de imagens, de luzes, de sons, de que entre elas não circule o vento, que sobre elas não chova, e de que, por exemplo, seja impossível esperar que nasça uma for dentro do o da palavra for. ... Mesmo

agora sentiu o cheiro das folhas molhadas e não sabe onde está a palavra que devia exprimir esse cheiro, essa folha e essa água. Uma só palavra para dizer tudo isto já que muitas não o conseguem. (56)

Such a "desabafo" as the narrator says is, on the one hand, a simple realization that words by themselves can never express experience in its totality, that there is always something lost. On the other hand, it is also a critique of representation, for the writer is not here advocating a medium that would be capable of better approximating reality, does not claim that a movie, for instance, would be capable of doing what writing cannot, because what is in question is the very nature of representation itself. Saramago does not go into the extreme of denying all value to representation, or of thinking that somehow it would be possible to avoid the representational, but he is very consciously alerting the reader to the need to always bear in mind how any project to represent reality must always assume its own limitations, in other words, that there can be no transparency.

One word Saramago uses to refer to his narrative, just mentioned in the passage cited, is that of register. This is significant inasmuch as Saramago's project is a double one, which at the same time that it reveals to the reader places outside the normal tourist routes, faces of Portugal with which not many will be familiar, and art treasures only a few will ever see, it also serves to inscribe them into memory. That is, time, a constant preoccupation throughout the narrative, is also an agent of destruction and not merely change, against which the narrative fights, by fixing places and objects. Saramago is well aware and often complains about the ravages of time and the incomprehensible way in which many treasures of Portugal's past are left to disappear. By writing about those places and those objects, Saramago is also creating a record, a memory of them, from which future generations might benefit if the original represented no longer exists. This is a concern that is also not without its problems. If Saramago's narrative, even as it creates a space for memory, avoids the pitfalls of memorialization, that is, avoids becoming a reactionary plea for conserving a static image of Portugal, at the same time his zeal to defend, to preserve, what he fears might be lost forever, also leads him to controversially argue for the removal of objects and monuments from their intended spaces into the sanctuary of the museum:

certos monumentos deveriam ser retirados do lugar onde se encontram e onde vão morrendo, e transportados pedra por pedra para grandes museus, edifícios dentro de edifícios, longe do sol natural e do vento, do frio e dos líquenes que corroem, mas preservados. Dir-lhe-ão que assim se embalsamariam as formas; responderá que assim se conservariam. (84)

Obviously Saramago himself is aware of the extreme state of such a position, which even contradicts his own attention to the way in which architecture is foremost a question of spatial integration. Although many other points concerning representation could be raised, I would like to bring up only one more because of the direct way in which it involves history, memory, and representation.

While describing Carvalhal de Óbidos, the traveler mentions that in a tower there was found a leather collar used to chain a slave, with the inscription: "'Este preto he de Agostinho de Lafetá do Carvalhal de Óbidos'" (275). After noting how the collar is said to have been taken to the archeological and ethnographic museum in Lisbon, Saramago promises that the first action he will do when visiting Lisbon will be to search for that collar. Indeed, upon entering Lisbon, the first thing the traveler mentions is finding the collar in the museum:

> O viajante repete uma vez e outra para que fique gravado nas memórias esquecidas. Este objecto, se é preciso dar-lhe um preço, vale milhões e milhões de contos, tanto como os Jerónimos aqui ao lado, a Torre de Belém, o palácio do presidente, os coches por junto e atacado, provavelmente toda a cidade de Lisboa. Esta coleira é mesmo uma coleira, repare-se bem, andou no pescoço dum homem, chupou-lhe o suor, e talvez algum sangue ... Agradece o viajante muito do seu coração quem recolheu e não destruiu a prova de um grande crime. (290)

The passage is somewhat hyperbolic but consistent with Saramago's position on history, his desire for a material history, and his aim to counter official history with the history of the dispossessed. As such, his claim that the collar, which testifies to the crime of slavery, is worth as much as the whole city of Lisbon, is an appropriate image for the way in which Lisbon, inasmuch as it was the capital of the empire, is the center for such crimes. Indeed, what Saramago focuses on in his description of Lisbon, even though it still remains somewhat attached to the sights a tourist would not want to miss, avoids romanticizing the city and does, indeed, focus on its people, either those of Alfama or those of Bairro Alto, as well as on the historic vicissitudes of a people who, even though they had to pay for the construction of the monumental aqueduct built to bring fresh water into the city, saw the record of such payment annulled by the governmental effacement of the original inscription (364–365). By emphasizing the need for collective memory to preserve the material records of the sufferings of the past, Saramago is also very consistent with his attempt throughout the narrative to de-center traditional history, to present indeed another perspective on the nation that, at the same time that it serves to ground pride on being Portuguese, avoids falling into the traps of nationalistic mythologies. And yet, one cannot but wonder why there are so few instances in which the traveler questions the role assumed by Portugal as imperial power, as a colonizing nation, why indeed they have to be concentrated in such few passages, such as the one mentioned. "Todo o viajante tem o direito de inventar as suas próprias geografias," (311) says the traveler at one point, but such choice also involves a responsibility (recognized by Saramago as a mediation between generations, 172), and that is why the reader might have expected, even among the difficulty of choice, some more critical involvement with what, after all, dominated Portugal and the idea of Portugal for most of its existence as a nation.

Viagem a Portugal is also a text that Saramago uses to put forward some notions about what travel means, and it is to these that I would like to turn as a form of conclusion. Travel is both internal and external, as has been mentioned. But beyond that, Saramago makes two fundamental distinctions. One involves the radical demarcation he would like to establish between himself and tourists, conscious as he is that to some, if not many, of the people he encounters he will be seen precisely as a tourist. This is a tempting demarcation but also a difficult one to establish. If Saramago is traveling with other intentions than those of the normal tourist, that is, if his principal aim is epistemological, as he himself remarks, he also notes that he falls short of his ideal of travel. For, even if he is not just intent on arriving at a place, if indeed what interests him are the detours and the travel itself for what he can find during it, he is also always without time, always finding it impossible to stay. In his words, to travel is to stay: "Que veio o viajante fazer à Nazaré? Que faz em todas as povoações e lugares onde entra? Olhar e passar, passar e olhar. Já se sangrou em saúde, já declarou que viajar não é isto, mas sim estar e ficar" (241). This observation is not as paradoxical as it seems, for what the traveler misses is the possibility of coming to know the people in the places he passes through, that is, coming to the point of empathy with them. As Caren Kaplan notes in her recent study of travel and displacement, "For many of us there is no possibility of staying at home in the conventional sense—that is, the world has changed to the point that those domestic, national, or marked spaces no longer exist."[5] Even if Saramago has not suffered the conditions of exile motivated by the wars that constantly erupt around the world fueled by the resurgence of bloody nationalisms, it is still in a sense that feeling of never reaching a point of being at home that is behind his comment on what travel should be and does not come to be, or behind his inability to answer the question about whether he is from Lisbon affirmatively: "O viajante, ás vezes, não sabe muito bem de que terra é, e por isso responde: 'Tenho andado por aí'"—a condition that is not as singular as it seems, as the answer from his interlocutor confirms: "'É o que acontece a todos nós'" (316).

At the conclusion of the narrative, Saramago still inserts a double negative, which attempts to pass for an affirmative statement. Having concluded the chapter before the last with the words, "este é o país do regresso. A viagem acabou," he must start the last short chapter by denying it: "Não é verdade. A viagem não acaba nunca. Só os viajantes acabam. E mesmo estes podem prolongar-se em memória, em lembrança, em narrativa" (387). And that is precisely the case of Saramago's narrative, of his role as traveler, of his image of Portugal, and of the invitation for us all to go on our own voyages.

NOTES

1. See, for instance, Boaventura de Sousa Santos, "Onze Teses por Ocasião de Mais uma Descoberta de Portugal," *Luso-Brazilian Review* 29.1 (1992): 97–115. And also Boaventura de Sousa Santos, "State and Society in Portugal," *After the Revolution: Twenty Years of Portuguese Literature, 1974–1994.* Ed. Helena Kaufman and Anna Klobucka, Bucknell University Press, Lewisburg; Associated University Presses, London, 1997, 31–74.

2. See *After the Revolution: Twenty Years of Portuguese Literature, 1974–1994, op. cit*; and *Literatura. Nacionalismos. Identidade*, a thematic issue of *Discursos* 13 (1996).

3. José Saramago, *Viagem a Portugal*, Caminho, Lisboa, 1995. Further references in the text will be to this, the 11th edition of the text without the photographs.

4. From a vast bibliography on travel writing, see George Van Den Abbeele, *Travel as Metaphor: From Montaigne to Rousseau*, University of Minnesota Press, Minneapolis, 1992.

5. *Questions of Travel: Postmodern Discourses of Displacement*, Duke University Press, Durham and London, 1996, p. 7.

ANDREW LAIRD

Death, Politics, Vision, and Fiction in Plato's Cave (After Saramago)

The novels of José Saramago, the Nobel Prize-winning author from Portugal, rely as much on spectacle as they do on speculation. The story of *Memorial do Convento* (1983), known to English readers as *Baltasar and Blimunda*, is set in the early 1700s, but its sermonizing narrator implicitly addresses us from the plateau of a communist utopia, as conceived by quite contemporary lights. The fiction itself is organized around a description of the construction of the vast Franciscan monastery at Mafra. That description is cumulatively developed, refined, and inlaid as Saramago unfolds the story of a fugitive priest who invents a flying machine. Speculation and spectacular fantasy again converge in *Jangada De Pedra* (1986), or *The Stone Raft*, which also employed an iconic scenario: the Iberian peninsula falls away from the Pyrenees, and thus from Europe, to run adrift in the Atlantic Ocean.

The issue of vision itself—or lack of it—is more acutely explored in Ensaio sobre a cegueira (1995), another dystopic novel by Saramago about the spread of blindness as a contagious disease. The title (Essay on Blindness) signals that this work is something more than a dark fantasy. It may be tempting to liken this achievement to the fictional-satirical scenarios of Voltaire, Swift, or Samuel Butler, but as an exploration of moral and political behavior, Saramago's work is not a polemic with an obvious target. The lack of a specifiable message endows the essay on blindness with a richer suggestive quality. This intractability hints at a greater philosophical depth:

From *Arion*, vol. 10, no. 3 (Winter 2003). © 2003 by Andrew Laird.

the work could even be compared to a Platonic myth in which enigma prevails over tidy allegory. Saramago's most recent novel, published in Lisbon in 2000 and just translated into English, provides a sounder endorsement for a comparison with Plato than one could have hoped for. It is entitled A Caverna, The Cave, and forms the final part of a triptych—of which Ensaio sobre a cegueira was the first, and the second a novel called Todos os nomes (1997).[1] A Caverna presents a political and philosophical vision of today's world, and points to its potential for transformation, for worse as well as for better. The complex relation A Caverna has to the account of the Cave in Plato's Republic will emerge in the following summary of Saramago's plot.

The main characters are an old man, Cipriano Algor, a traditional potter whose business is in decline, his daughter Marta Isasca, and her husband, Marcial Gacho. Marcial is employed as a security guard in the Center, a new model city within a city, in which people both live and work. Shopping, recreational, residential, and entertainment facilities are all provided within the Center so that its members have no need to leave. Marcial's job is insecure, and he aspires for it to be made permanent so that he can be offered an apartment in the Center. He tries to persuade his father-in-law, who is relatively content with his life and with his trade in pottery, to apply to move into the Center with him and Marta. However, Cipriano Algor is told by the Center that they do not want to market his pottery because the demand for such items is already met by the manufacture of plates and cups from synthetic materials. Moreover, he is compelled to collect and destroy his work because the rules of the Center prohibit him from selling it anywhere else. So Cipriano, with the help of his daughter, instead turns his talent to producing little clay figures of people. The Center at first expresses interest in the figurines, although the old man is daunted by the fact that he would have to produce a run of several thousand. However, the models are finally rejected and so must be destroyed, but not before Cipriano has hidden six prototypes in a cavern beneath the Center for whenever they might be needed.

The three members of the family move to the Center but shortly afterwards the news spreads of a sinister occurrence which is being kept secret. Something very serious has been found underneath the Center. As a security guard, Marcial Gacho is aware of what it is, but he is bound by his job not to reveal anything to his wife and father-in-law. Cipriano defies orders by going down to the entrance of the cave below the Center where his son-in-law is standing guard. Marcial at first rebukes him but in the end gives Cipriano a lantern and lets him enter the cave to see what the authorities have been so keen to conceal. The old man makes his way down a gently inclining slope dimly illuminated by the light of the fire burning at the top. At the bottom, there are six human corpses, tied by their legs and necks to a stone bench so that they are facing a wall. The bodies are still distinguishable as three men and three women but their eyes have completely rotted away.

Cipriano Algor makes his way back to the entrance and asks Marcial for his view of the significance of what they have seen. His son-in-law says, "Some time ago I read of something like this." Cipriano says that although the bodies are palpable—he touched one of them—they are not actually real and that they are somehow a reflection of the world outside. He senses that the scenario is a kind of call from the future: the corpses are to be identified with himself, Marcial, Marta, the inhabitants of the Center, perhaps with the whole world. Cipriano explains the whole situation to his daughter and announces to his family that he is determined to leave the Center immediately, no matter how uncertain the prospects outside might be. The others finally agree to join him. When they have made some progress on their journey, they recall a sign on the front façade of the Center. The father and daughter who are both illiterate ask Marcial what it said. Marcial Gacho's reply, which he gives as if he is reciting from memory, constitutes the last sentence of Saramago's novel: "Coming soon: the opening to the public of Plato's Cave, exclusive attraction, unique in the world, buy your entrance ticket now."

A Caverna can be regarded as a reformulation of Plato's text. It can be seen as a contemporary contextualization, as a political allegory, or simply as an amplification of the passage in the *Republic*. Saramago's story can no less effectively be read as an etiology or "prequel" for Plato's description. Even though, for the purposes of this discussion, I plan to use *A Caverna* as a kind of commentary on Plato, as a hermeneutic tool for finding some ways to interpret the Cave, it would certainly be tempting to reverse the process, and to use Plato to elucidate Saramago. But the purpose of this essay will be to deal with the important facets of Plato's Cave which are excavated by *A Caverna*: death, politics, vision, and fiction.

DEATH

For Cipriano Algor, the humans he finds in the cave, terrible as they are to discover, are not real. Nor are they are real for us as readers. But is their non-reality for us the same as their non-reality for Cipriano Algor? The problem of not-being goes to the heart of what fiction is and involves. It is also specifically addressed in a different way by Plato's *Sophist*, but in his Cave and in the *Republic* this question also bears on the issue of fictionality. Yet in addition to not being real—whatever that might mean—the occupants of Saramago's cave are dead. This is not true—or at least not true in the same way—of the occupants of Plato's Cave who are sentient, and who can think after a fashion (*nomizein* and *bêgeisthai* are the verbs used) and talk to each other. However a quotation of Achilles' words from the *katabasis* (or journey to the Underworld) in *Odyssey* 11 gives pause for thought. Socrates applies these words to the prisoner who has escaped from the Cave to the world above at 516d: "he would much prefer being a slave laboring for someone else— someone without property" than to think and live like the people in the Cave. This quotation is apt because Achilles in making that remark was contrasting the world of shadows (*skiai*) in Hades with the world of human life. Socrates famously comments on the same Homeric passage earlier, when he expounded on censorship of poetry, at the beginning of book 3 of the *Republic*:

> We shall start by wiping out of the epic all the lines like these:
> I would rather be a slave working for someone else
> Someone without property, who had a small livelihood
> Than to rule over all the dead that have perished.

However, Socrates did go on to say there that such conceits and expressions "might be useful for some other purpose" (387c)—and it is perhaps here, in his elaboration of the condition—of the Cave, that we see what this purpose is.

The conception of the Cave as domain of death—in opposition to the super-terranean realm of vision—is soon reinforced by a second Homeric echo at 516e. Socrates wants Glaucon to imagine the former prisoner coming out of the sunlight reassuming his place in the Cave, and asks

> ἆρ᾽ οὐ σκότους ἂν ἀνάπλεως σχοίη τοὺς ὀφθαλμούς;

> Would his eyes be full of darkness?

This expression recalls diction used on numerous occasions for characters who die in the *Iliad*. Those Homeric expressions about the blindness of death are frequently, and not that surprisingly, accompanied by the falling, or downward movement of the character in demise:[2]

> τὸν δὲ σκότος ὄσσε κάλυψεν,
> ἤριπε δε, ὡς ὅτε πύργος, ἐνὶ κρατερῇ ὑσμίνῃ.

Darkness covered his eyes and *he fell*, like a wall in mighty conflict.

> (*Iliad* 4.461–2)

τὸν δὲ σκότος ὄσσε κάλυψε,
δούπησεν δὲ πεσών

Darkness covered his eyes and *he fell* with a thud.

> (*Iliad* 4.503–4)

ἐκ δ᾽ ἄρα πᾶσαι
χύντο χαμαὶ χολάδες, τὸν δὲ σκότος ὄσσε κάλυψε.

And *down to the ground poured* all his guts, and darkness enfolded his eyes.

> (*Iliad* 4.525–6 = 21.180–2)

ἤριπεδ᾽ ἐξ ὀχέων, στυγερὸς δ᾽ ἄρα μιν σκότος εἷλεν

He fell from the chariot, and darkness took him.

> (*Iliad* 5.47)

δούπησεν δὲ πεσών, τὸν δὲ σκότος ὄσσε κάλυψε.

He fell with a thud and darkness covered his eyes.

> (*Iliad* 15.578)

That frequent association of darkness with death, however, contributes to the resonance of Socrates' question here. The association between the Cave and Hades is underlined by the invitation later made by Socrates to Glaucon to discuss the education of the Philosopher Kings at 521c:

Βούλει οὖν τοῦτ᾽ ἤδη σκοπῶμεν, τίνα τρόπον οἱ τοιοῦτοι ἐγγενήσονται, καὶ πῶς τις ἀνάξει αὐτοὺς εἰς φῶς, ὥσπερ ἐξ Ἅιδου λέγονται δή τινες εἰς θεοὺς ἀνελθεῖν;

Would you like us to look next at how to produce people of this type in our community, and how to lead them up to the light—like the people we hear about who rise from Hades to dwell among the gods?

POLITICS

As well as with death, Saramago's novel also shows how Plato's Cave might be linked with questions of politics. It is not difficult to see a political allegory in *A Caverna*: the Center, as a glorified shopping mall containing en suite accommodation, with all the disturbing allure it has for Marcial Gacho, clearly symbolizes the excesses of monopoly capitalism, which are nowadays as undisguised as they are unrestrained. Or rather, the Center might be said to *depict* such excesses directly. After all, a North American entrepreneur, by the name of Norm Nixon, is currently fanfaring the imminent launching of the so-called *Freedom Ship* from the coast of Florida. This will be the largest ocean-going vessel ever built, containing helipads, shopping precincts, and multi-million dollar apartments. As both a symbol and a material bastion of free-floating market forces, this Leviathan is supposed to be sailing the world's seas by 2008, rendering any notion of the "ship of state" a dead metaphor, to say the least.[3]

In Saramago's novel, there is no end to the deceitful illusion of the gigantic commercial Center which is one of the two worlds presented in the book; the other world, emblematized by Cipriano Algor's pottery workshop, is in a rapid state of decline. The workshop represents a way of life which is less and less under our control, as plant and animal species become extinct, professions become redundant, languages lose their speakers, and traditions lose their meaning. But, as is always the case with atrocities and catastrophic phases in human history, it is unwise to try too rapidly to identify the heroes and villains of any scenario before apportioning blame. Onlookers, witnesses, apparently neutral parties, not to mention captives themselves, tend to collude with the captors. No reader of *A Caverna* can fail to associate the figurines Cipriano Algor made and placed in the cave under the Center with the six corpses he later discovers there, at the climax of the story. The association is not made explicit, but it does not need to be: Marcial Gacho is not the only collaborator; his father-in-law himself is responsible for fashioning, like a demiurge, the very models that come to represent the predicament he and his family end up seeking to escape.

Although the *Republic* in general is understood as essentially an inquiry into justice and the nature of social organization, Plato's account of the Cave itself tends to be conceived exclusively as an exploration of truth and reality. The Cave is conventionally regarded as helping to set out the metaphysical and epistemological foundations which underlie the discussions of moral and social issues in surrounding parts of the dialogue. The Cave episode itself is not normally read or interpreted politically—or at least political interpretation of it never seems to go beyond appreciating the obvious point that the illustration is concerned with the philosopher's education and its significance to society. Even appreciation of that point alone seems fairly limited: many of today's philosophically-minded readers of Plato are prone to see the Sun, Line, and Cave as somehow detachable from the socio-political concerns of the text in which they feature. These illustrations are in fact seamlessly integrated into the whole as numerous passages serve to show, and as C.D.C. Reeve's book *Philosopher-Kings* (1988), highlighting the coherence of the *Republic*'s argument, helps to demonstrate—even if one does not share Reeve's view of what the principal emphases of that argument are.

However, a way in which the Cave alone might reflect a political scenario *tout court* is suggested by the famous model of the *camera obscura* set out by Karl Marx and Friedrich Engels in *The German Ideology*. The basic idea is in the Preface:

> If in all ideology men and their relations appear upside down as in a camera obscura, this phenomenon arises just as much from their historical life-process as the inversion of objects on the retina does from their physical life-process.

A useful account of Marx's figure of the *camera obscura* and of the concept of commodity as a fetish or idol is provided in the final chapter of *Iconology: Image, Text, Ideology* by W.J.T. Mitchell (Chicago 1985). That chapter indicates the suggestive richness of these metaphors, and attempts, by drawing from Raymond Williams, Fredric Jameson, and E.P. Thompson's critique of Althusser, to show how they have had a counteractive effect on Marxist thought, as the "concreteness" of ideology and fetishism have become disengaged and abstracted from historical specificity and dialectic. To put it glibly, the concept of fetish has become fetishized and "ideology" has become idealized. But what is of most concern here, though, is the affinity between the way Marx attempts to make concrete the notions of ideology and commodity and the fiction in the *Republic*. Mitchell remarks:

> If we think of the camera obscura as a figurative descendant of Plato's Cave with its shadows projected on the wall, the fetishes are like the objects that cast the shadows, [in Plato's words], "human images and shapes of animals as well, wrought in stone and wood and every material." The standard interpretation of the allegory of the Cave might easily be applied to Marx as well: "The artificial objects correspond to the things of sense and

opinion ... and the shadows to the world of reflections, *eikones*."
In the interplay of these things and reflections arises a dialectic—
an idealist one in Plato's case, a materialist one in Marx's.

This is an affinity which could be explored in greater depth. The model of
dialectic in *The German Ideology* radically diverges from the Platonic one: for
Marx and Engels dialectic is grounded in materialist presuppositions that
appear completely contrary to those of the Platonic Socrates. Yet at the same
time, the convergence between the pictorial vehicles of their respective
systems is further exposed in the following paragraph from the *The German
Ideology*:

> In direct contrast to German philosophy which descends from
> heaven to earth, we ascend from earth to heaven. That is to say,
> we do not set out from what men, say, imagine, conceive, nor
> from men as narrated, thought of, imagined, conceived, in order
> to arrive at men in the flesh. We set out from real, active men,
> and on the basis of their real-life process we demonstrate the
> ideological reflexes and echoes of this life process. The phantoms
> formed in the human brain are also, necessarily, sublimates of
> their material life-process, which is empirically verifiable and
> bound to material premises.

Towards the end of *The German Ideology*, it is conceded that some individuals
are able to be liberated from their "local narrow-mindedness," *not* as a result
of thinking themselves into a new position, but as a result of "their empirical
reality and owing to empirical needs": a capitalist going bankrupt would be a
crude example. Such "favorable circumstances," as Marx cheerfully calls
them, are historically specific and exceptional. The possibility of such
unexpected liberation (which is initially unpleasant for the individual
concerned) is obviously comparable to the liberation Socrates conceives for
the prisoner who is forced out of the Cave in *Republic* 515–16:

> And if someone dragged him forcibly away from there up the
> rough, steep slope and didn't release him until he'd pulled him
> out into the sunlight, wouldn't this treatment cause him pain and
> distress?

The crucial fact that the prisoner's eventual coming to his senses does not
depend on his own doing should alert to us to some important things.

First, a significant feature of diction runs directly in tension with the scenario of the Cave generated in the opening of *Republic* 7. Language of coercion and compulsion is used by Socrates for the *freeing* of the prisoners, but not for the detailed account of their being held and bound in the first place which runs from 514a to 515c4. We should remember that the word *desmôtês* first used by Socrates at 514b4 overwhelmingly connotes someone in bonds. That connotation is underscored by the precise description Socrates gives of the way the *desmôtai* are bound up. Thus the conventional translation of "prisoner" risks importing excess baggage; "captive" or "bondsman" are better translations for *desmôtês*.

Yet once Socrates embarks on encouraging Glaucon to imagine the inhabitants of the Cave being *freed* from their physical bonds, his diction is peppered with terms conveying force and control. At 515c6, for instance, he verges on oxymoron: "When one was *freed and compelled* (λυθείη καὶ ἀναγκάζοιτο) to stand up suddenly" (515c6).[4] The fact that Glaucon himself, in a response to the initial scene Socrates is sketching, uses the word "compelled" (ἠναγκάσμενοι) for the occupants of the Cave at 515b1 only shows that he is unaware of the game being played. The irony of this is delicately enhanced by words Plato uses for two subsequent affirmative answers Glaucon gives to Socrates. First at 515b6, his retort "Inevitably" (in Greek, this is *anagkê*, which is strictly a noun, "compulsion"); and shortly afterwards again at 515c2 Glaucon says "Absolutely inevitable" (again in Greek *pollê anagkê* literally means "much compulsion"). Incidentally, the personified *Anagkê* appears in the Myth of Er, having usurped the place of Moira or Fate—she is even equipped with her spindle. An exploration of the political implications of the relation between *anagkê* and *douleia* ("servitude") was long ago provided by George Thomson in his book *The First Philosophers* (1955). Yet the deployment of such diction of coercion and its rhetorical effect in the Cave seems to have gone unnoticed in all the literature on this part of the *Republic*. Overall, this diction draws attention to the involvement of an external agent in the liberation of the captive from the Cave. The identity of that agent is not clear but it does point to a social dimension of Socrates' illustration which is not always recognized.

The extent of human involvement and complicity in engineering the environment of the Cave in the first place is made abundantly clear at the beginning of Socrates' description in 514b–515a:

> "A low wall has been built, just like those conjurors have, which is placed in front of the *people* (ἀνθρώπων), above which they put on their shows (θαύματα)."

"I see," he said.

"See also then on the other side of this wall *people* (ἀνθρώπους) carrying all kinds of equipment rising above the wall: statues of humans and various animals, crafted in wood and stone and all sorts of materials—typically some of the men doing the carrying will be talking, and others will be silent."

A note in Adam's commentary on the *Republic* (1902) argues decisively, if it needs to be argued, that these *anthrôpoi* or "people" are the orchestrators of the show, and not the spectators. This human involvement is one thing which makes Plato's cave different from what we know of its major precursor in Greek literature, as well as from its successors. Empedocles sees our world as a dark place of punishment compared with the realm of the gods. For him, according to Porphyry and Proclus at least, that whole world in which we live is a cavern—and mortals can have no part as captors in constructing or maintaining it:

καὶ οἱ Πυθαγόρειοι καὶ μετὰ τούτους Πλάτων ἄντρον καὶ
ὀπήλαιον τὸν κόσμον ἀπεφήναντο. παρά τε γὰρ᾽ Ἐμπεδοκλεῖ αἱ
ψυχοπομποὶ δυνάμεις λέγουσιν·"ἠλύθομεν τόδ᾽ ὑπ᾽ ὑπόστεγον."

The Pythagoreans and after them Plato presented the world as a
cave and cavern. And in Empedocles the powers that escort souls
say: "We have come under this covered place ..."
                    (Porphyry, *On the Cave of the Nymphs 9*
                    [= Empedocles fr. B120 D–K])

                         ἀτερπέα χῶρον,
ἔνθα Φόνος τε Κότος τε καὶ ἄλλων ἔθνεα Κηρῶν
αὐχμηραί τε Νόσοι καὶ Σήψιες ἔργα τε ῥενστὰ
Ἄτης ἂν λειμῶνα κατὰ σκότος ἠλάσκουσιν.

a joyless place where Killing and Rancor and other tribes of
Doom, parching Diseases and Rots and deeds of flux wander
through the dark on the meadow of Madness
                    (Empedocles fr. B121 D–K)

But where the Cave as the centerpiece of the *Republic* is concerned, it is difficult not to sense some kind of political signification. A little later on in 519d we find the word *desmôtai* having a broader application: referring to those members of society who need help from founders of the state, to the end of binding the community together. Later still in book 9, Socrates endows the notion of captivity with a new and rather unexpected political spin, as he outlines the unhappy lot of the tyrant at 579b:

> And is it not in *such a prison-house the tyrant is bound* (δεσμωτηρίῳ δέδεται ὁ τύραννος) being by nature such as we have described, full of numerous varied fears and desires? For him alone of those in the city, greedy in soul as he is, it is neither at all possible to travel around nor *to see all those festivals* (θεωρῆσαι) which other free men are keen to see.

There is a specific point: the deprivation of sight-seeing conveyed by the word *theôrêsai* here forges a connection between this predicament of statecraft and philosophical vision which will recur, once we address the role of the Cave as a *mise-en-abyme* for the text of the *Republic*. But, more generally, it goes without saying that long after Plato, romantic poets and post-enlightenment philosophers continued to charge the palpable imagery of bondage and captivity with a more universal political significance. More recently, in *Soledad Brother* (1970) and *Blood in my Eye* (1971), George Jackson viewed the power structures and hierarchies of race in the Californian prison system he experienced—the "world" directly accessible to him—as a paradigm for a critique, on the macrocosmic level, of North American society as a whole.

One more issue related to questions of vision bears on this endeavor to politicize the Cave, although it has a much broader significance. The notion of "ideology," coined by Destutt de Tracy in 1801, which originally denoted a "science of ideas" revealing to people the foundations of their beliefs, was rooted in visual paradigms and analogies involving optical instruments like mirrors and telescopes. Marx and Engels, as noted above, inherited this vehicle to attack the proposition that ideas can change or shape reality, and to argue that all ideas are socially determined. But as well as being widely used in a weaker sense to label a plain system of thought, "ideology" has been defined in cultural theory as a scheme social groups use to make the world more intelligible. A still more neutral version propounded by Clifford Geertz, presents ideology as a necessary "symbolic map" which can replace traditional cultural symbol systems (such as religion or science) which may have broken down.[5] And Michel Foucault went so far as to unite the stronger and weaker senses of the term: for him ideology is akin to epistemology—it reflects a desire for an ideal knowledge, free of error and illusion.

The Greeks evidently showed a grasp of ideology in the weak sense—religious doctrines, philosophical schools, political allegiances, ruler cults—but did they entertain the notion of ideology in any stronger sense? To ascribe to the ancients anything like our post-enlightenment science of ideas would at first seem to be a gross anachronism. However, the formulations of Geertz and Foucault show that the potential for slippage between *ideas* and *theories of ideas* is always there. Plato's attempts to expose the hazards of opinion (*doxa*) as opposed to true knowledge (*epistêmê*) beg a similar question to those begged by de Tracy and Marx: what is the critical force of calling someone else's position ideological? Theories of ideas end up becoming ideas themselves—just as specific ideas can provide the architecture for grander system building. This slippage is recognized in Plato's *Republic*, which is even more of a study in the *theory* of ideology than it is a study of epistemology and political philosophy.

And the slippage is reflected by the Cave, and by the way this visually-oriented account of the transition from illusion to knowledge is embedded in the dialogue. The inhabitants of the Cave are preoccupied with the projected *shadows* of stone or wood figurines which they confuse with the objects they portray: they are not directly confusing the figurines themselves with those objects. This is notoriously problematic if we try to harmonize precisely the way the ascendance towards knowledge is illustrated here with the hierarchy in Socrates' preceding model of the Line which extends from the realm of perceptual thought to understanding: as I.M. Crombie pointed out in 1962, "we should [then] make Socrates say that the general condition of mankind is that of looking at shadows and reflections" (*An Examination of Plato's Doctrines*, 117). Various solutions which have been offered to make the two models fit together will be bypassed here in order to consider the upshot of Socrates' own explication of the Cave at 517b:

> This *image* (*eikôn*) ... should be applied as a whole to what was said before, likening the region presented through sight to the prison-dwelling, and the light of the fire in it to the power of the sun. And if you assume that the ascent and the contemplation of the things above is the soul's ascension to the intelligible region, you'll not be wrong about what is my hope at any rate, since you desire to hear it. But only God knows if it happens to be true. But the *impression* I have is that *apparently* the last thing to be seen—and it is hardly seen—is the idea of the good ...

Here we can see that Socrates, never mind Plato, is very far from holding that the truth is something to which he has any access: he can only express his desire for that ideal knowledge free from error and illusion. The Cave which at first seemed to provide an alluring visual model for the *theory* of the ideas we hold—a model which sought to take us beyond our mistaken ideas and assumptions—has become in turn nothing more than just another idea. And a similar sentiment is articulated again after the next occasion on which Socrates rehearses the illustration of the Cave. He then responds to Glaucon's questions about the role of dialectic as a way to the end of their enquiry at 533a:

> You will no longer be able to follow—though there is no lack of enthusiasm on my part—and you would no longer see an image of what we are talking about, but the truth itself, what at any rate appears as the truth to me. Whether it really is or not, this is not any longer worth insisting on, but to see something like this is to be insisted upon.

Notwithstanding the caricaturing of Platonism by contemporary philosophers like Richard Rorty, these two passages at least would seem to square with the claims of Rorty's own neo-pragmatism: that ultimately there are no firm foundations which epistemology can use to discriminate between different systems of belief.[6] Those passages which each come in the context of Socrates' retrospective comments on the Cave show that in his view this paragon, which is supposed to be both the symbol and validation of Platonic idealism, also reveals its limitations. When all is said and done, epistemology falls into phenomenology, knowledge becomes a matter of insistence or affirmation, and truth, even with its image discarded, can only be something apparent to the viewer.

VISION

The reflections above lead to the question of the Cave itself as an image. On a couple of occasions I have non-committally referred to the Cave as an "illustration," although it would be preferable to have avoided such a characterization. Philosophers, critics, and translators of Plato habitually refer to the "parable" or "allegory" of the Cave, although none of the Greek equivalents of such terms is used in the *Republic* at least. Maybe there is nothing particularly wrong with calling the Cave an allegory. Still this informality is surprising when scholars of very different persuasions have gone to such lengths to discriminate between terms like *muthos* and *logos*, and to assess the relation between them in Plato's own usage.[7] In his essay "Plato's Doctrine of Truth" (1932), Martin Heidegger referred to the "allegory of the Cave," but he was crafty enough to employ quotation marks whenever he did so. In *Les Mythes de Platon* (1930) Percéval Frutiger actually provided a defense of the term "allegory" which is curious: the Cave is an allegory and should not be confused with a myth because, Frutiger claimed, it does not represent a series of events but a static condition.

In the text of the *Republic* however, the Cave is consistently referred to as an *eikôn*. Socrates heralds the whole scene at the beginning of book 7 as follows:

> *Compare* (ἀπείκασον) our nature in respect of our education and lack of it to an experience like this. *Imagine* (ἰδὲ) men in an underground cavernous dwelling ...

Glaucon's response to the scenario Socrates presents is to say:

> Ἄτοπον, ἔφη, λέγεις εἰκόνα

> It is an unusual *eikôn* you are speaking of ...

The verb used for the imperative "compare" (*apeikazein*) can also be used to convey the notion of *forming a model*, copying in painting as well as expressing a likeness in words; and the noun *eikôn* in fifth century literature customarily means a physical image or likeness, whether a picture or a statue. However, Aristophanes uses the term to signify a similitude or comparison:[8]

> τὰς εἰκοὺς τῶν ἐγχέλεων τὰς ἐμὰς μιμούμενοι

> those copying my comparisons involving eels
> (Aristophanes, *Clouds* 559)

>   οὕτω δ᾽ ὅπως ἐρεῖτον
> ἀστεῖα καὶ μήτ᾽ εἰκόνας μήθ᾽ οἷ᾽ ἂν ἄλλος εἴποι

> both speak elegantly, and no similes or things someone else might say.
> (Aristophanes, *Frogs* 905–6)

And in the passage 517a–b already quoted, the use of *eikôn* clearly has the sense of "comparison ":[9]

> This image (*eikôn*) [Socrates says there] should be applied as a whole to what was said before, likening the region presented through sight to the prison-dwelling, and the light of the fire in it to the power of the sun.

Here the scene of the Cave is presented effectively as the vehicle of a simile. The trouble is that for the tenor of the simile we are asked to go a bit further back in the dialogue. By "what was said before" (τοῖς ἔμπροσθεν λεγομένοις), Socrates seems to mean the account of sight and the sun which was itself characterized as an *eikôn* in 509a—an image (or a comparison) which he there asked Glaucon to *scrutinize* (ἐπισκόπει) as if it was an actual object of vision. This recursiveness is fascinating but it is also rather annoying. It would have been a lot more convenient for me if it had been applied in another way which can be briefly outlined.

Basically, if it had been the case that at any point in the account of the Cave the illusory shadows of objects surveyed by its inhabitants had been called *eikones*—if that had happened just once—life would have been easier. We would have had a scenario reminiscent of Carlos Fuentes' derisive account of small town life in Iowa, where every Saturday night, regular teenage couples consume popcorn and coke, as they gawp at a movie screen which depicts regular teenage couples consuming popcorn and coke, as they gawp at a movie screen and so on, *ad infinitum*.[10] Something like that would have been clever and it would have gone nicely with the mischievous claim made earlier that Plato put the Cave there to signal the limitations of philosophical idealism. But as it is, the complexity of the category of eikôn prohibits such an easy resolution.

However, Plato does at least play a figurative game with the notion of *eikôn* elsewhere in the *Republic*, earlier at 487e–488a. Socrates explains to Adeimantus that the question he is asking requires an *eikôn* by way of reply. "I don't think you're accustomed to use *eikones* in what you say" is Adeimantus' sarcastic reaction. Socrates' response to this is not only to reply with his habitual iconic analogy but to use another *eikôn* to characterize the one he says he is compelled to produce: a figure of painters who make goat-stags and other hybrid animals—an image which is of course vengefully meta-iconic in itself.

As well as "comparison" or "analogy," *eikôn* can of course mean a "model" or "likeness." This kind of connotation is certainly to be found in Plato where models can have immensely varying relations to their objects. For instance we are told in *Timaeus* 37d that time is an *eikôn* of eternity; in the *Cratylus* that names can be *eikones* of what they designate; and in the *Philebus* 39b–c that *eikones* are pictures painted in the soul as souvenirs of assertions we make. That last instance involving memory must have some relation to the link between *eikones* in Plato and the recollection of Forms which we apprehended before birth. Crucially, though, it is Aristotle who gives much more legitimacy than Plato to the use of *eikones* in thought and memory—for him all thinking requires images (*De Memoria et Reminiscientia* 449b; *De Anima* 431a, 431b, 432a). For Plato, it is dialectical thought that is needed to bring out that recollection, and not the use of images, as is made very clear in the *Republic* at 510b, 511c and 532a. Even so, given the kind of thing Socrates says in *Phaedo* 72d–e and elsewhere—"coming to life again is a fact and it is a fact that the living come from the dead and that the souls of the dead exist"—it is tempting to think about the extent to which the *eikôn* of the Cave with its undertones of *katabasis*, could represent a kind of recollection in that regard.

Socrates' very disdain for the *eikôn* as an instrument of proper thought makes it just as tempting to consider the Cave itself as a perversely successful kind of mnemotechnic *topos*. Although Socrates uses the word *topos* of the Cave itself apparently in a routine sense, Glaucon calls the illustration of the Cave an *atopos eikôn*! Socrates' fashion of constructing this particular *eikon* is certainly in line with the recommendation in Aristotle's treatise on memory at 452a12 that a *place* (*topos*) makes a good starting point (*archê*) for recollection. And it is worth recalling Cicero's *De Oratore* 1.354, the *locus classicus* on the art of memory, if only because of the relevant emphasis that passage puts on likenesses and effigies. The Cave was designed to be remembered within the dialogue or Socrates would not keep harking back to it. And going beyond its recurrences in the text of the *Republic*, the presence of the Cave in the collective memory of our popular culture is as powerful as its impact on the memory of any individual reader of Plato.[11]

These issues open up numerous cans of worms and it is debatable how far interpretation of the word *eikôn* in the *Republic* should be subject to interference from alien usages of the term—even when they are drawn from other Platonic dialogues. However, that does not mean that, by confining our scrutiny of the term to the *Republic* alone, we can conveniently circumscribe its meaning (and by implication fix the role of the Cave in the rhetorical organization of the work). Even though the word *eikôn* can generally be taken, within this dialogue, to denote "comparison" alone, it has at least as many nuances as there are varieties of comparison. And it is worth quoting a sentence at 401b where the term seems to have a different sense:

> Is it then only the poets we must stand over and compel to *embody* (ἐμποιεῖν) in their poems the *eikôn* of good character or else not to write poetry among us, or must we stand watch over the other craftsmen and forbid them to embody bad, character...?

After this all too rapid survey of the suggestive possibilities of the word *eikôn* as Plato's own term for the Cave, calling it an "allegory" makes everything look far too cosy and tidy. Moreover, terms like "allegory" import all kinds of baggage which contain further problems of their own. It is easier to side with Socrates: to conceive of the Cave as an *eikôn* helps to describe, explain—and give freer rein to—much of its generative power.

FICTION

This generative power bears on fiction—not only on specific examples such as Saramago's *A Caverna*, but on the category of fiction as a whole. The influence of Platonic dialogue on the evolution of fictional forms and ideas both in antiquity and beyond is immeasurable.[12] This was long ago recognized by Mikhail Bakhtin, Erwin Rohde, and far more grudgingly, by Friedrich Nietzsche, at one time a close friend of Rohde. However, I am less interested in the purely formal and typological aspects of this influence, and more interested in the role Plato's work highlights for philosophy itself as a *practice* in the evolution and conception of what is now deemed fiction. The interface between philosophy and fictional fabrication on the one hand, and between social performance (storytelling or philosophizing) and production of texts on the other is a key concern—especially in the wake of *Genres in Dialogue* (1995), Andrea Nightingale's important book on the construction of philosophy through the Platonic dialogue. And as vision (or spectacle) is very much bound up with the relationship between philosophy and fiction, the historical and theoretical insights promised by Nightingale's forthcoming work on the philosophic gaze will also have a major bearing on the observations to follow.

The Cave is a central focus for these concerns about the relation between philosophy and fiction in several ways: one can see its presence, with varying degrees of intensity, in ancient texts of various kinds, which are now,

for better or worse, firmly classified as "fiction." The influence of the Cave
on an episode in Lucian's *True Stories* is particularly striking when the
narrator recounts his experience of being inside the body of a whale:

> ἐπεὶ δὲ ἔνδον ἦμεν, τὸ μὲν πρῶτον σκότος ἦν καὶ οὐδὲν
> ἑωρῶμεν, ὕστερον δὲ αὐτοῦ ἀναχανόντος εἴδομεν κύτος μέγα
> καὶ πάντη πλατὺ καὶ ὑψηλόν, ἱκανὸν μυριάνδρῳ πόλει
> ἐνοικεῖν.

> When we got inside it was dark at first and we could see nothing;
> later on however when the whale opened its jaws we saw a great
> *cavern*, broad in every direction and high, big enough to hold a
> large city.
>
> (True Stories 1.31)

The influence is no less conspicuous as the description, which plays on the
words for a "cavern" (*kutos*) and "whale" (*kêtos*), continues:

> καὶ ὅλως ἐῴκειμεν τοῖς ἐν δεσμωτηρίῳ μεγάλῳ καὶ ἀθύκτῳ
> τρυφῶσι καὶ λελυμένοις. Ἐνιαυτὸν μὲν οὖν καὶ μῆνας ὀκτὼ
> τοῦτον διήγομεν τὸν τρόπον ... ἅπαξ γὰρ δὴ τοῦτο κατὰ τὴν
> ὥραν ἑκάστην ἐποίει τὸ κῆτος, ὥστε ἡμᾶς πρὸς τὰς ἀνοίξεις
> τεκμαίρεσθαι τὰς ὥρας.

> Altogether we resembled men in a great prison where we were
> free to live an easy life but from which we could not escape. This
> was how we lived for one year and eight months ... the whale
> opened his mouth once an hour you see, and that was how we
> told the time.[13]
>
> (True Stories 1.39–40)

But it is possible to go further: Lucian's sketch in fact serves to "excavate" and
bring to prominence—more than even Porphyry's allegory—the fictional
dynamic of Socrates' *eikôn* as a vehicle of philosophical thought and even as
a *mise en abyme* for the mimetic endeavor of the *Republic* as a whole. Lucian
seems to engage far more thoroughly with this than is often realized. And in
Apuleius' *The Golden* Ass, a cave provides the location for Charite's captivity
in 4.22, where she is entertained with the specifically Platonic allegory of
Cupid and Psyche in which Psyche herself descends to the underworld. The
conditions of Plato's Cave are evoked elsewhere in the *The Golden Ass*—for

instance the *ekphrasis* in the second book where the narrator Lucius is absorbed in the reflected image of the carving of Diana and Actaeon. That is presented as a comment on his own predicament: "*Tua sunt cuncta quae vides*," he is told. Even Petronius' account of the dinner of Trimalchio in the *Satyricon* contains resonances of the Cave which remain to be explored. John Bodel's analysis of the *Katabasismotiv* in that scene in relation to the social status of the freedmen certainly endorses a political reading of the Cave as Petronius' intertext.[14]

Why does the Cave recur in works like these? We could dismiss this recurrence as routine literary *imitatio*: produced either by authors as a form of allusion, or, if you prefer the intertextual model, by readers. But instances of *imitatio* like this are never routine: if they were, they would not prompt comment. One might just as well ask why the Cave would *not* recur in works like these. In fact that might be a better question to ask given that Plato's Cave all at once involves philosophy, fiction, and vision. However distinct these contemporary categories may be for us in general terms, they are not separable elements or distinct ingredients when it comes to consideration of the *eikôn* of the Cave. Each of them is a perspective, a way of conceiving an indivisible, primordial whole. It might be salutary to wonder whether, without Plato's Cave, or at least, without Plato, those texts in which the Cave figures as a cameo (and many others like them) would have come to exist in the first place.

Demonstrating the extent to which philosophy, fiction, and vision are interdependent in the Cave would mean starting this essay all over again. To avoid getting tangled up, one can make the same sort of point by reviewing a passage earlier in the *Republic* which I have considered in depth elsewhere.[15] In the debate about justice, Glaucon thus introduces his story about the ancestor of Gyges who found a ring which could make people invisible:

> As for the fact that people only ever do good unwillingly out of the inability to do wrong—we would most clearly perceive this, if we made the following thought experiment. Suppose we grant each type of person—just and unjust—the license to do whatever he wants, and we then follow each of them in our gaze to where desire will lead them. We'll catch our just person red-handed: his desire for superiority will point him in the same direction as the unjust person, towards a destination which every creature naturally regards as good and aims for, except that people are compelled by convention to deviate from this path and respect equality. They'd have the kind of license I am talking about

especially if they acquired the kind of power which, they say, an
ancestor of Gyges of Lydia once acquired ...

(359b–c)

A number of expressions used here show how the very process of
philosophical thought becomes expressed in fictional discourse. The phrase
(toionde poiesamen te dianoia) translated here as "if we made the following
thought experiment," literally means "if we made something like this in
thought." The verb *poiein* is celebratedly used for poetic fabrication. Glaucon
says that the making of something in thought ensures we "most clearly
perceive" his point—that people only ever do good unwillingly, out of their
inability to do wrong. The scenario he proposes is thus figured as a
manufactured projection, which once we have produced it, we can then *look
at* and learn from. Intellectual contemplation and gazing are connoted by
theasthai; the participle form employed here routinely serves as a noun
meaning "spectators"; and the connection with *theôria*—"theory" is well
known.

To conceive of the initial scenario as a *spectacle* involves a leap of
imagination as well as intellect. That scenario then takes a more specific
shape: the story to come is really a refinement, a more precise qualification
of the simple idea Glaucon first posits: "They'd have the kind of license I am
talking about," he explains, "especially if they acquired the kind of power
which, they say, an ancestor of Gyges of Lydia once acquired ..." Glaucon, in
effect, transforms a hypothesis devised for the sake of argument into an act
of conjury: a philosophical speculation is taking us into a fictional situation.
The connections between the full blown story, even as it develops, and its
genesis in philosophical argument are never lost: the emphases on vision,
sight, and perception in the tale of the ring themselves reflexively connect
the fiction with its function. These emphases hint at an implicit analogy
between the ancestor of Gyges who beholds the marvels in the story and the
story's teller and audience who scrutinize the story and its protagonist's
behavior. Thus iconicity *in* the tale is bound up with the iconicity *of* the tale
as an object of philosophical speculation and as a virtual spectacle.

Such "hypericonicity" becomes increasingly prevalent in literature
after Plato: reflexive accounts of *descriptio* and *ekphrasis* abound in ancient
poetic and rhetorical theory and mnemotechnical loci provide numerous
examples. It is possible that such meta-*ekphrasis* might have had some part to
play in the formation of invented fiction as a genre: the Chinese-box effect
in the opening of Longus' *Daphnis and Chloe* is one example. Overall the
embedding of Glaucon's tale indicates not merely a parallel, but an intimate

involvement between philosophical thought and the creation of a fabulous scenario. (Significantly the ring story is invented by Plato: the resemblance it has to Herodotus' account of Gyges actually helps to demonstrate this). But in the Cave, philosophical speculation and fictional spectacle go even beyond that intimate involvement to enjoy a relation of identity. This is partly because the hypericon of the Cave is more autonomous: billed enigmatically as an *eikôn*, it is not a thought experiment which is ancillary to an argument—as an experience to which Socrates asks us to liken our "nature" (*phusis*), it in fact sets the agenda for arguments to follow.

The Cave is a fiction but it is also an exploration of fiction and a vehicle of fiction, just as we saw that it could be an idea in itself as well as an exploration of ideas people hold. If one is skeptical about the claim that the Cave exhibits a preoccupation with its own fictionality, it is worth considering again Glaucon's comment at 515a on the initial scenario Socrates unfolds and Socrates' response to him:

"Ἄτοπον, ἔφη, λέγεις εἰκόνα καὶ δεσμώτας ἀτόπους.
Ὁμοίους ἡμῖν, ἡμῖν, ἦν δ᾽ ἐγώ.

"A strange *eikôn*," he said "you are presenting and strange captives."
"They are just like us," I said.

By saying that the captives are just like himself and Glaucon, Socrates is normally taken to be making a point about human life in general. Robin Waterfield, in a note on his English translation of the *Republic*, puts it baldly: "This statement is unequivocal evidence that the Cave is an *allegory* ... we do not spend our lives literally gazing at shadows of artefacts."[16] That comment may or may not be well and good. But there could be another dimension to Socrates' point if one does not take the word ἡμῖν ("us") to refer to a general "us," all of us as humans. "Us" could instead refer specifically to Socrates and his companions in the dialogue *as* characters in the dialogue. Being mere characters in a craftily constructed *mimesis*, Socrates' friends live in the trap, which most readers have fallen into at this point, of thinking that they, and all that they see and hear are real.

This instructive, almost Brechtian form of romantic irony suggests that the Cave could be a *mise en abyme* for the *Republic* as a whole. Certain aspects of the dialogue's composition support this: the programmatic opening and first word *katebên* ("I went down") which has been seen to prefigure the philosopher's descent to the Cave as well as the myth of Er, could signal descent into a mimetic, fictional realm as much as a plunge into the mythical world of *katabasis*.[17] Demetrius and Quintilian both tell us Plato spent a great deal of time writing the first words of the *Republic*. And vision is involved in the *mise en abyme* as well: the opening of the text extensively deals with the spectacular attractions of the celebration for the goddess Bendis—a festival taking place in the dark of night and involving a horseback torch race.

Debates in analytic philosophy about logical closure and the nature of the reality of fictional worlds are inextricably bound up with debates about logic and truth in our own world. But those debates ignore other moral and political questions that can be raised by the kind of contemplation of fictionality prompted by the Cave. The following comment by Hannah Arendt in *The Human Condition* (1958)—though prompted by her reading of Plato's *Laws*—is very pertinent here:

> The Platonic god is but a symbol for the fact that real stories, in distinction from those we invent, have no author; as such, he is the true forerunner of Providence, the "invisible hand," Nature, the "world spirit," class interest, and the like with which ... philosophers of history tried to solve the perplexing problem that although history owes its existence to men, it is still obviously not "made" by them.[18]

Finally, the current fascination classicists have with vision, with spectacle, with the gaze, might partly be due to the misconception that, unlike reading, discourse, language, rhetoric, identity, gender, and power, the notion of the gaze can be fixed. The hope that we might be able to reconstruct ancient modes of viewing is enticing but it is futile.[19] Certainly a resurgent preoccupation with reconstruction in general has led to an increasing dominance of the so-called "cultural historical" approach to interpreting ancient literature, Greek literature in particular. There is nothing intrinsically wrong with such an approach as long as its application is strictly provisional, but there is with its potential dominance to the exclusion of other approaches. The institution of a new brand of positivism in classical studies by a kind of velvet revolution should not go unchallenged.

In the face of such tendencies, the Cave is a useful interdisciplinary talisman. It shows the inevitable slippage between vision and the theory of vision, between fiction and the theory of fiction, between ideas and the theory of ideas, and even between history and the theory of history. Moreover, how one reads the Cave is bound up with how one reads the *Republic* as a whole—a text in which Socrates shows full awareness of the fact that the content of poetry and other forms of discourse is actualized by performance. And because the Cave exposes the slippage between reading and the theory of reading, its function in the *Republic* will never be determined. Plato's Cave is a cliché, but it can also be reassuring in helping us to see our way through, or beyond, a difficult, unreadable world.

NOTES

Various conversations led to this paper: I would like to thank António Passos Leite, Margarita Manresa Clemente, Maria De Caldas Antao, and especially Xon de Ros. I am also grateful to the Classics department at Stanford for inviting me to present this material to the Visual Literacies Workshop in April 2001.

1. *A Caverna* (Lisbon 2000); Spanish translation, P. del Rio (Madrid 2001); English translation, Margaret Jull Costa (New York 2002). The pictorial connotations of the word "triptych" are appropriate.

2. In addition to the passages quoted here, see *Iliad* 6.11, 13.575, 14.519, 13.672, 16.607,16.325, 16.316, 20.393, 20.471.

3. The project's objectives, as stated on the website (http://www.freedomship.com) in November 2001, are to "create a vigorous commercial community whose privately owned and operated on board enterprises will sell their products and services world-wide and operate totally free of local taxes and duties" and to "establish the world's largest duty-free retail shopping mall."

4. Compare also: ἀναγκαζοι ("one should compel") at 515d5 and again at 515e1, as well as me μὴ ἀνείη ("not release") and βία ("by force") 515e7.

5. Clifford Geertz, *The Interpretation of Cultures* (New York 1975).

6. See Richard Rorty, *Consequences of Pragmatism* (Brighton 1982) and *Philosophy and Social Hope* (Harmondsworth 1999), a more recent collection of philosophical and political essays.

7. See e.g., Luc Brisson, *Platon: les mots et les mythes* (Paris 1982); P. Murray "What is a *Muthos* for Plato?" in R. Buxton (ed.), *Studies in the Development of Greek Thought* (Oxford 1998), 251–62; K. Morgan, *Myth and Philosophy from the Presocratics to Plato* (Cambridge 2000).

8. Compare Aristotle *Rhetoric* 1407a10. See also M. McCall, *Ancient Rhetorical Theories of Simile and Comparison* (Cambridge, MA 1969) and M.S. Silk, *Interaction in Poetic Imagery* (Cambridge 1974).

9. Compare also the use of *eikôn* to mean "analogy" in *Republic* 375d and 538c.

10. Carlos Fuentes, *Diana o la cazadora solitaria* (Mexico 1994).

11. Films like *Pleasantville* (dir. G. Ross 1998) and *The Matrix* (dir. L. and A. Wachowski 1999) are recent examples. The passages assembled by Konrad Gaiser in *Il paragone della caverna: Uariazioni da Platone a oggi* (Naples 1985) give some impression of the *Nachleben* of the Cave from late antiquity onwards.

12. The *Republic's* relation to contemporary poetics, assessed in a chapter entitled "Platonic Formalism: Socrates and the Narratologists" in my book, *Powers of Expression, Expressions of Power* (Oxford 1999), is just one facet of this influence.

13. Compare Plato *Rep.* 514a–18b, esp. 514, 516a–d.

14. J. Bodel, "Trimalchio's Underworld" in J. Tatum (ed.), *The Search for the Ancient Novel* (Baltimore 1994), 232–59.

15. A. Laird, "Ringing the Changes on Gyges: Philosophy and the Formation of Fiction in Plato's *Republic*," *Journal of Hellenic Studies* 12.1 (2.001), 12–29.

16. R. Waterfield, *Plato Republic: A New Translation* (Oxford 1993), 423.

17. M. Burnyeat, "First Words: A Valedictory Lecture," *Proceedings of the Cambridge Philological Society* 43 (1997), 1–20, especially 5–8.

18. *The Human Condition* (Chicago 1958), 185. Hannah Arendt continues: "Nothing in fact indicates more clearly the political nature of history—its being a story of action and deeds rather than of trends and forces or ideas—than the introduction of an invisible actor behind the scenes whom we find in all philosophies of history which for this reason alone can be recognized as political philosophies in disguise."

19. Much recent work on *ekphrasis* has of course engaged in this pursuit. See (for example) J. Elsner (ed.), *Art and Text in Roman Culture* (Cambridge 1996).

Chronology

1922	Born on November 16 to José de Sousa and Maria de Piedade, landless peasants in Azinhaga, a small village in the province of Ribatejo, north of Lisbon.
1936	Family moves into its first house; Saramago goes to school, but parents cannot afford to send him for very long. Studies mechanics at a technical school for five years and then works in a car repair shop for two years.
1944	Marries Ilda Reis.
1947	His child, Violante, is born. Publishes first novel, *The Land of Sin*.
Late 1950s	Production manager of a Lisbon publishing company, Estúdios Cor, until 1971; as a result, becomes friends with important Portuguese writers.
1966	Returns to the literary scene after 19 years when he publishes *Os poemas possíveis* (*Possible Poems*).
1967–1968	Works as a literary critic.
1969	Joins the then-illegal Communist Party.
1970	Divorced from wife. Publishes another book of poems, *Provavelmente Alegria* (*Probably Joy*).
1971	Publishes *Deste mundo e do outro* (*From this World and the Other*), a collection of newspaper articles. Works for the next two years as an editor and the manager of a cultural supplement at the newspaper *Diário de Lisboa*.

1973	Publishes *A bagagem do viajante* (*The Traveller's Baggage*), a collection of newspaper articles.
1975	Beomes deputy director of the newspaper *Diário de Noticias*. Fired from newspaper.
1975–1980	Supports himself as a translator.
1979	Publishes a play, *The Night*.
1980	Publishes *Levantado do chao* (*Risen from the Ground*, also translated as *Raised from the Ground*) and *Que farei com este livro?* (*What Shall I Do with This Book?*).
1981	*Viagem a Portugal* is published (later published in English in 2001 as *Journey to Portugal*).
1982	*Memorial do convento* (in English as *Baltasar and Blimunda*) is published. Adopts it for the libretto of the opera *Blimunda*, first performed in 1990.
1984	*O ano da morte de Ricardo Reis* (*The Year of the Death of Ricardo Reis*) is published.
1986	*A jangada de pedra* (*The Stone Raft*) is published.
1987	Publishes *A segunda vida de Francisco de Assisi* (*The Second Life of Francis of Assisi*).
1988	Marries the Spanish journalist Pilar del Rio.
1989	*História do Cerco de Lisboa* (*The History of the Siege of Lisbon*) is published.
1991	*O Evangelho segundo Jesus Cristo* (*The Gospel According to Jesus Christ*) is published. After the Portuguese government voices opposition to the book (which it later retracts), he leaves Portugal to live in the Canary Islands with his wife.
1995	*Eusaio sobre a Cegueira* (*Blindness*) is published.
1997	*Todos os nomes* (*All the Names*) is published.
1998	Receives Nobel Prize for Literature, the first Portuguese-language author to do so.
1999	*Conto da ilha descohecida* (*The Tale of the Unknown Island*) is published.
2000	*La Caverna* is published. (Translated into English the following year as *The Cave*.)

Contributors

HAROLD BLOOM is Sterling Professor of the Humanities at Yale University. He is the author of over 20 books, including *Shelley's Mythmaking* (1959), *The Visionary Company* (1961), *Blake's Apocalypse* (1963), *Yeats* (1970), *A Map of Misreading* (1975), *Kabbalah and Criticism* (1975), *Agon: Toward a Theory of Revisionism* (1982), *The American Religion* (1992), *The Western Canon* (1994), and *Omens of Millennium: The Gnosis of Angels, Dreams, and Resurrection* (1996). *The Anxiety of Influence* (1973) sets forth Professor Bloom's provocative theory of the literary relationships between the great writers and their predecessors. His most recent books include *Shakespeare: The Invention of the Human* (1998), a 1998 National Book Award finalist, *How to Read and Why* (2000), *Genius: A Mosaic of One Hundred Exemplary Creative Minds* (2002), and *Hamlet: Poem Unlimited* (2003). In 1999, Professor Bloom received the prestigious American Academy of Arts and Letters Gold Medal for Criticism, and in 2002 he received the Catalonia International Prize.

RICHARD A. PRETO-RODAS is Professor of Romance Languages and Literatures in the Division of Language and Linguistics at the University of South Florida in Tampa, where he has also been director of the division. He is the author of several books and articles pertaining to the literature of Portugal, Spain, and Brazil, and also a joint editor of several titles in this genre. He also serves as a reviewer or review editor for numerous journals.

MARY L. DANIEL has taught at the University of Wisconsin at Madison. She is the author of *Trollope-To-Reader*.

GENE STEVEN FORREST has taught at Southern Methodist University.

GIOVANNI PONTIERO, now deceased, taught at the University of Manchester. He was an editor and joint editor and translated many books, including several by Saramago.

DAVID FRIER teaches at the University of Leeds in the United Kingdom, where he has also been Departmental Advisor to Research Students. He writes extensively on Saramago and plans to publish a monograph on him. He is the author of *Visions of the Self in the Novels of Camilo Castelo Branco*.

MARK J.L. SABINE teaches in the Department of Hispanic and Latin American Studies at the University of Nottingham.

RONALD W. SOUSA is Professor of Portuguese, Spanish, and Comparative Literature at the University of Illinois, Champaign-Urbana. He is the author of *The Rediscoverers, Major Writers in the Portuguese Literature of National Regeneration* and co-author of *The Humanities in Dispute*. He has also translated into English several works of literature and literary theory.

PAULO DE MEDEIROS has been Professor and Chair of Portuguese Studies at the University of Utrecht, Holland. He is the author of *Delectable Structures: Consumption and Textuality in the Western Civilization* and of many articles in various journals.

ANDREW LAIRD has been Reader in Latin Literature at Warwick University in the United Kingdom. He is the author of *Powers of Expression, Expressions of Power: Speech Presentation and Latin Literature*.

Bibliography

Arnaut, Ana Paula. "The Subversion of History in *Memorial do Convento*." *Portuguese Studies* 15 (1999): 182–193.

Bloom, Harold. "'The One with the Beard Is God, the Other Is the Devil.'" *Portuguese Literary and Cultural Studies* 6 (Spring 2001): 155–166.

Cerdeira da Silva, Teresa Cristina, and Anna Klobucka. "On the Labyrinth of Text, or, Writing as the Site of Memory." *Portuguese Literary and Cultural Studies* 6 (Spring 2001): 73–96.

Costa, Horácio. "The Fundamental Re-Writing: Religious Texts and Contemporary Narrative: Gore Vidal's *Live from Golgotha*; Salman Rushdie's *The Satanic Verses*; José Saramago's *O Evangelho Segundo Jesus Cristo*." *Dedalus* 6 (1996): 245–253.

———. "The Fundamental Re-Writing: Religious Texts and Contemporary Narrative: Gore Vidal's *Live from Golgotha*; Salman Rushdie's *The Satanic Verses*; José Saramago's *O Evangelho Segundo Jesus Cristo*." *Poligrafías* 1 (1996): 189–198.

Costa, Horácio, and Kimberly Da Costa Holton. "Saramago's Construction of Fictional Characters: From *Terra do Pecado* to *Baltasar and Blimunda*." *Portuguese Literary and Cultural Studies* 6 (Spring 2001): 33–48.

Daniel, M.L. "Ebb and Flow: Place as Pretext in the Novels of José Saramago." *Luso-Brazilian Review* (Winter 1990).

Ferreira, Ana Paula. "Cruising Gender in the Eighties: From *Levantado do Chão* to *The History of the Siege of Lisbon*." *Portuguese Literary and*

Cultural Studies 6 (Spring 2001): 222–238.

Fokkema, Douwe. "How to Decide Whether *Memorial do Convento* by José Saramago Is or Is Not a Postmodernist Novel." *Dedalus* 1 (1991): 293–302.

France, Peter, ed. *The Oxford Guide to Literature in English Translation*. New York: Oxford University Press, 2001.

Frier, David G. "José Saramago's *Stone Boat*: Celtic Analogues and Popular Mythology." *Portuguese Studies* 15 (1999): 194–206.

Grossegesse, Orlando. "Journey to the Iberian God: Antonio Machado Revisited by Saramago." *Portuguese Literary and Cultural Studies* 6 (Spring 2001): 167–184.

Kaufman, Helena, and Anna Klobucka, eds. *After the Revolution: Twenty Years of Portuguese Literature, 1974–1994*. Bucknell University Press, Lewisburg; Associated University Presses, London, 1997.

Klobucka, Anna. "Introduction: Saramago's World." *Portuguese Literary and Cultural Studies* 6 (Spring 2001): xii-xxi.

Krabbenhoft, Kenneth. "Saramago, Cognitive Estrangement, and Original Sin?" *Portuguese Literary and Cultural Studies* 6 (Spring 2001): 123–136.

Lough, Francis. "National Identity and Historiography in José Saramago's *A Jangada de Pedra*." *Tesserae* 8, no. 2 (December 2002): 153–163.

McNee, Malcolm. "An Intertextual Intertwining of Mystic Nationalism: Saramago's Post-Modern Challenge to the Pessoan and Salazarist Discourses in *O Ano da Morte de Ricardo Reis*." *Lucero* 10 (Spring 1999): 57–66.

Monteiro, George. "The Bureaucratic Tale of the Harbor Master and the Collector of Customs." *Portuguese Literary and Cultural Studies* 6 (Spring 2001): 239–243.

Pontiero, Giovanni. "Embargo." *Cimarron Review* 110 (January 1995): 10–18.

———. "José Saramago." *Bulletin of Hispanic Studies* 71, no. 1 (January 1994): 115–148.

Preto-Rodas, Richard A. "José Saramago: Art for Reason's Sake." *World Literature Today* 73, no 1 (Winter 1999): 11–18.

Riding, A. "A Writer With an Ear for the Melody of Peasant Speech: The New Nobel Prize Winner José Saramago Trains an Outsider's Irony on Time, Faith and History." *The New York Times* Section E (December 28, 1998).

Sabine, Mark. "'Once but no longer the prow of Europe': National Identity and Portuguese Destiny in José Saramago's *The Stone Raft*." *Portuguese Literary and Cultural Studies* 6 (Spring 2001): 182–203.

———. "Re-Incarnating the Poet: Pessoa, the Body and Society in José Saramago's *O ano da morte de Ricardo Reis*." *Journal of Romance Studies* 2, no. 2 (Summer 2002): 37–52.

Saramago, José. "The Art of Fiction CLV: Conversation with 1998 Nobel Prize for Literature Laureate Jose Saramago." Interview by Donzelino Barroso. *Paris Review*, 149 (Winter 1998): 54–73.

———. "Interview with José Saramago." Interview by Giovanni Pontiero. *PN Review* 16, no. 4 (1989): 38–42.

Seixo, Maria Alzira. "The Edge of Darkness, or, Why Saramago Has Never Written about the Colonial War in Africa." *Portuguese Literary and Cultural Studies* 6 (Spring 2001): 205–219.

Tamen, Miguel, and Helena Carvalho Buescu. *A Revisionary History of Portuguese Literature*. New York: Garland Publishing, 1998.

White, Hayden. *The Content of the Form: Narrative Discourse and Historical Representation*. Baltimore: The Johns Hopkins University Press, 1987.

Acknowledgments

"A View of Eighteenth-Century Portugal: José Saramago's *Memorial do convento*" by Richard A. Preto-Rodas. From *World Literature Today* 61, no. 1 (Winter 1987): 27–31. ©1987 by *World Literature Today*. Reprinted by permission. www.ou.edu/worldlit.

"Symbolism and Synchronicity: José Saramago's *Jangada de Pedra*" by Mary L. Daniel. From *Hispania* 74, no. 3 (September 1991): 536–541. ©1991 by The American Association of Teachers of Spanish and Portuguese, Inc. Reprinted by permission.

"The Dialectics of History in Two Dramas of José Saramago" by Gene Steven Forrest. From *Hispanófila* 106 (September 1992): 59–68. ©1992 by *Hispanófila*. Reprinted by permission.

"José Saramago and *O Ano da Morte de Ricardo Reis*: The Making of a Masterpiece" by Giovanni Pontiero. From *Bulletin of Hispanic Studies* 71, no. 1 (January 1994): 139–148. ©1994 by Liverpool University Press. Reprinted by permission of Taylor & Francis Ltd.

"Ascent and Consent: Hierarchy and Popular Emancipation in the Novels of José Saramago" by David Frier. From *Bulletin of Hispanic Studies* 71, no. 1 (January 1994): 125–138. ©1994 by Liverpool University Press. Reprinted by permission of Taylor & Francis Ltd.

"The One with the Beard is God, the Other is the Devil" by Harold Bloom. From *Portuguese Literary & Cultural Studies 6. On Saramago* (Spring 2001): 155–166. © 2001 by the University of Massachusetts Dartmouth.

"Once but no longer the prow of Europe": National Identity and Portuguese Destiny in José Saramago's *The Stone Raft* by Mark J.L. Sabine. From *Portuguese Literary & Cultural Studies 6. On Saramago* (Spring 2001): 185–203. © 2001 by the University of Massachusetts Dartmouth.

"José Saramago 'Revises,' Or Out of Africa and Into Cyber-History" by Ronald W. Sousa. From *Discourse* 22, no. 3 (Fall 2000): 73–86. ©2001 by Wayne State University Press. Reprinted with the permission of Wayne State University Press.

"Invitation to the Voyage" by Paulo de Medeiros. From *Global Impact of the Portuguese Language*, edited by Asela Rodriguez de Laguna: 167–178. ©2001 by Transaction Publishers. Reprinted by permission.

"Death, Politics, Vision, and Fiction in Plato's Cave (After Saramago)" by Andrew Laird. From *Arion* 10, no. 3 (Winter 2003): 1–30. ©2003 by Andrew Laird. Reprinted by permission of the author.

Index